A Spirituality of Fundraising

Workbook Edition

Henri J. M. Nouwen
with Nathan Ball

UPPER
ROOM BOOKS®
NASHVILLE

Unless otherwise indicated, scripture quotations are from the New Revised Standard Version Bible, copyright © 1989, Division of Christian Education of the National Council of Churches of Christ in the United States of America. Used by permission. All rights reserved.

Scripture quotations designated NJB are taken from The New Jerusalem Bible, copyright © 1985 by Darton, Longman & Todd, Ltd. and Doubleday, a division of Random House, Inc. Reprinted by permission.

Cover design: Sue Smith and Pearson & Co.
Interior design: PerfecType | Nashville, TN
Cover art: Gogh, Vincent van, (1888). *The Sower*. Erich Lessing / Art Resource, NY

Print ISBN: 978-0-8358-1880-3 | Mobi ISBN: 978-0-8358-1881-0 | Epub ISBN: 978-0-8358-1882-7

Printed in the United States of America

For Timothy Ball (1960–1984) and Jean Vanier (1928–2019)
and all others who strive to live from the heart.

CONTENTS

ACKNOWLEDGMENTS

On September 16, 1992, four years before his untimely death in 1996, Henri Nouwen gave an informal talk to the Marguerite Bourgeoys Family Service Foundation on spirituality and fundraising. Sister Sue Mosteller, Henri's literary executrix, knew that Henri's talk was a treasure that needed to be made widely available.

In April 2003, Sue turned to John Mogabgab, Henri's former teaching, research, and editorial assistant at Yale Divinity School, and asked if he would transform the transcript of Henri's talk into a text for publication. John's abundant skills as a writer and editor, his close working relationship and friendship with Henri, and the fact that Henri regularly granted John the liberty to add material to Henri's ideas made John the perfect person for the job. Like a master potter, John took Henri's ideas and words and shaped them into a beautiful and durable text that continues to help fundraisers today. Sue, John, and I had fun dreaming about the publication of Henri's text and joyfully worked together, along with Pamela Hawkins and Robin Pippin, to produce *A Spirituality of Fundraising*.

Fifteen years later, in 2018, Karen Pascal, Executive Director of the Henri Nouwen Society, asked me to reflect on Henri's text and my own experience of fundraising and to write a workbook that included *A Spirituality of Fundraising*. This workbook edition stands on the shoulders of Henri himself and the wisdom and service of the people who brought its first printing into being.

The ideas in the workbook are inspired by Henri, by my own experiences, and by people who have influenced me over time. I have integrated learning from various sources that I gained while pursuing the work of fundraising. I thank all who have helped me whether by example or by offering advice or by teaching. My deepest desire is that Henri's text and my reflections will inspire others to go deeper into the relationship between spirituality and fundraising and that readers will share their insights and practices with the general public.

In terms of the writing process, I first want to thank Sue Mosteller. There is so much that I would not have done in my life had it not been for her love and support, this project included. My always honest and creative literary critics, Beth Porter and Tamara Yates, were, at various times, thought partners and needed cheerleaders. Thank you so much, each of you.

Fundraising from the heart is a road less traveled, and I have gleaned from the modeling and guidance of various people. I thank Dean Levitt, Richard Rooney, Hans Brenninkmeyer, Curt Armstrong, Heather Coogan, Chapman and Grace Taylor, Stephen Rothrock, Nick Fellers, Robb Pike, Alicia von Stamwitz, Nancy Stanfield, James Hoey, Jenifer McCrea, Jean Vanier, Michael Christianson, Mary Ruppert, and Ellen Eischen, all of whom have helped me along the way. Each of you has helped shape my thinking and experience of how to create friendships, partnerships, and communities of love within the context of fundraising.

I said yes to this writing project knowing that my life was already full of the challenges of raising four teenagers and a demanding new role that involves travel. Joanna Bradley Kennedy, my editor, paid the price as I broke one writing deadline after another. I thank her for her patience and for reviewing the manuscript with her careful eye.

Finally, a big thank you to the people who know the best and the worst of what I offer to the world: Timothy, Brendan, Anna-Claire, Emma, and my wife and partner, Paula.

INTRODUCTION

Fundraising is an incredibly important, often misunderstood, and notoriously difficult task for many people. Reading Henri Nouwen's beautiful little book *A Spirituality of Fundraising* and taking a deep dive into his vision through the accompanying workbook has the power to motivate you to embrace fundraising in a holistic way—as a positive, life-giving, and deeply human and spiritual task. Regardless of your fundraising experience or religious background, Henri's vision will energize and motivate you. Henri will help you to access the inner resources and confidence that you need in order to say "yes" to the task of fundraising.

A Spirituality of Fundraising is not a "how-to" book. Henri was not an expert on developing the various skills and practices often employed by people who fundraise. Instead, Henri's credibility came from his profound understanding of the heart. He knew its contours. Of course, I don't mean the organ that pumps blood throughout the body but the intangible place at the center of a person's being where will, emotion, mind, and perception come together. Henri described the heart as "the central and unifying organ of our personal life."[1] In Henri's Judeo-Christian tradition, the heart represents the spiritual core of a person, the mystical center of his or her existence. Henri experienced and reflected upon the deepest human motivations and emotions—the good, the bad, and the ugly—and he made it his life's work to guide and help others along life's journey.

Each of Henri's books explores one aspect or another of the inner life and the way of the heart. The central theme of Henri's writing is that our human and spiritual journey must be one of letting go of the illusion that our identity can be found in what we do, how much money we have or give away, or what others think of us. Living a spiritual life, says Henri, is fundamentally about claiming and reclaiming the truth of our eternal belovedness and allowing the inner voice of love to be the compass that directs our thoughts, words, and actions. Whether asking or giving, the ground of our common humanity and our life's work is to accept the "call to be deeply, deeply connected with Unconditional Love, with [our] own fragile humanity, and with brothers and sisters everywhere."[2]

But how does this belovedness relate to fundraising? Henri's great gift to us is showing us that fundraising is, first and foremost, a matter of the heart. Fundraising is about human connection. From the perspective of the gospel, it is about our connection with self, God, neighbor, and the world around us. Henri asserts that our fundraising will lack freedom unless we do the work of grounding ourselves in an experience of Divine Love. In *A Spirituality of Fundraising*, Henri concerns himself with the spiritual formation of both those who ask for money and those who give.

Henri's insight is important because our biggest blocks to fundraising are emotional and spiritual. This is not easily acknowledged. We might imagine that our resistance to fundraising lies in our just not being cut out for it or in not knowing what to do or in our fear of rejection. These are important issues. Skills are important, of course, but the source of our struggle is often deeper. We can read dozens of books on fundraising and still be left gasping for air when it comes time to ask for money. Reading Henri's book and spending time with Henri's insights as we move through the workbook will give us the air that we need.

My first response to the invitation to write a workbook to accompany Henri's text was that there must be someone else who could do this better than I. Although I have been a fundraiser for many years and have successfully asked people for money numerous times—sometimes for two hundred dollars and sometimes for two million—I am not a rockstar fundraiser. I continue to find that asking people for money awakens a feeling of vulnerability within me. Learning to ask with confidence in a manner that is authentic took time and is still an area of growth for me.

However, I said yes to writing a workbook for Henri's *A Spirituality of Fundraising* for two reasons. First, I knew Henri as a close friend and colleague over a ten-year period before he died. His spirit remains strong and present to me. I believe that the combination of our friendship and his profound influence on my life will help me illuminate his message. Second, I believe that my own difficulty with fundraising will help others who also struggle. Sharing a little about my personal journey as a fundraiser may give others greater confidence.

———

I've spoken with many people who have read Henri's book. Carolyn leads a social justice committee for her church. She confided in me, "I have always struggled with my relationship to money, but after reading Henri's book, I have a different perspective. I want to go deeper and reflect more, but already I feel inspired, less fearful, and even hopeful about my ability to ask for money. I am more ready to trust my inner sense of call and to find the freedom to invite others to invest financially in our vision."

Peter is a successful business person who knows a great deal about money and investing and who spends his free time contributing to a nonprofit group that does excellent work. He told me that, notwithstanding his business success and the high quality of the nonprofit organization, he has always been reluctant to ask people for money for the work of the latter. "Henri's book opened me to think differently," he said. "I want to learn how to apply his concepts practically."

This workbook edition of Henri's book is for them—and for you. It is designed to help you do the inner work necessary to understand your relationship with money and to guide you through the first practical steps that must be taken by anyone who wants to raise money. Its goal is that you and, perhaps, others in a group with whom you may meet will become more confident, competent, and successful in raising money for the causes that matter to you. This impact can come whether you have a paid role in which fundraising is one of your responsibilities or you serve as a volunteer. The workbook systematically explores Henri's main themes to help you address issues and soul questions that may be part of your fundraising journey. It will help you employ Henri's teaching effectively.

We each have a deep desire to grow into the fullness of who we can be and to make our best contribution toward a world in which love and justice flow freely. Henri showed me—and, I believe, he can show you—that fundraising is a privileged way of doing just that.

How I Came to Know Henri

Before you launch into this combined edition of Henri's text and workbook, I want to describe briefly how Henri and I came to know each other and how his friendship, teaching, and mentoring shaped both who I am and the fundraising work that I do.

Henri and I met in September 1984 in a small French village called Trosly-Breuil, north of Paris. Each of us had come to live in the original L'Arche community founded by Jean Vanier. In L'Arche, people with and without intellectual disabilities live and work together in small intentional communities. The purpose of L'Arche is to see the beauty of every person and to help one another, amid our own abilities and disabilities, to live confident, joyful lives.

L'Arche witnesses to the power of love in community and to the human transformation that can occur when people with differences—different intellectual ability, social status, ethnic and religious background, and economic access—share life together and develop authentic relationships. Some might describe L'Arche as an ongoing experiment in how people can grow in their capacity to give and receive love. It is no wonder, perhaps, that, after fifty-some years, L'Arche exists in forty countries around the world. Its existence testifies to a global thirst for places of belonging and love.

Henri had moved to L'Arche from Boston to begin a sabbatical year away from Harvard University. I was grieving the recent death of my youngest brother, was undecided about beginning graduate school, and had just joined the Catholic church after being raised in the Baptist tradition. I hoped that L'Arche would be a place where I could serve and, at the same time, find help in integrating the past and discovering a path forward. Henri and I were unlikely friends. He was Dutch and an accomplished intellectual. I was Canadian and a high-school dropout who had recently completed an undergraduate degree after a late entry into college. Henri was an extroverted, popular public figure. I was introverted and unsure of my direction in life.

Henri and I met far away from our respective homes in a foreign country and at a time when we both were searching for the next step in our lives. We quickly discovered that the same burning questions had led us to L'Arche: *What does it mean for me to live a more faithful spiritual life today? How is the Spirit of God calling me? What work shall I do, and where shall I live?* We were both excited to be part of L'Arche, curious about the mutual friendship to which we were drawn, and eager to support each other during this time of discernment. We had long conversations about the "project" of living in and helping to build intentional, mission-based community. We each knew that our time in France would be temporary, but neither of us could sense what would come next. We could not ever have imagined that for the next twelve years, our inner and outer lives would become interwoven as we discovered a mutual call to friendship and separate calls to become part of the mission of L'Arche on a permanent basis. Within a year, we each moved from France to L'Arche Daybreak, the first L'Arche community in North America, located just north of Toronto.

Henri joined the L'Arche Daybreak community as pastor and writer-in-residence and lived in the Dayspring, L'Arche's small house of prayer and meditation. I began a graduate degree in theology at Regis College, the Jesuit school at the University of Toronto, and lived in one of L'Arche's community homes. In 1990, I was invited to the role of Community Leader and Executive Director of L'Arche Daybreak. For the next six years, Henri and I worked side by side in our respective leadership roles, in service of the mission of L'Arche.

Almost twenty years ago, after a decade of leadership within L'Arche Daybreak and several years after Henri's death, I was asked to launch a new national fundraising function for L'Arche in Canada. I took on the project because I felt deeply called by the people and mission of L'Arche. My initial excitement was tempered when I realized that I was quite uncomfortable asking people for money. It wasn't just that I did not know, for example, how to tell the story of L'Arche effectively and when to ask for money. I also lacked an inner spiritual confidence—the knowledge that what I was doing as a fundraiser could bring me closer to other people and to God and that those who were investing financially in L'Arche could be equally blessed. My dominant early feeling was, *I wish we didn't have to do fundraising!* Because of Henri's writing on fundraising and my friendship with him, Henri played a huge role in helping me embrace fundraising as a mission; as a calling; and as an opportunity for storytelling, building community, and aligning strategies for change. Fundraising has taken me to the heart of my mission with L'Arche.

After fundraising in Canada for ten years, I spent five years as the Executive Director of the L'Arche International Foundation. In this role, I continued to work as a fundraiser, and I also did some training and consulting with L'Arche fundraisers and volunteers in central and western Europe, the United Kingdom, India, and Central and South America. It was not an easy time to be a fundraiser in L'Arche because we had not yet integrated fundraising into our mission. Although we knew that fundraising was necessary if we were going to accomplish our mission, there was a great deal of ambiguity and awkwardness about fundraising in our organizational culture. This is a common issue for many organizations. Happily, we were able to make the commitment and do the needed hard work to fully embrace fundraising as an indispensable aspect of our mission. I also learned during that time that, notwithstanding some differing emphases for cultural reasons, the vision, principles, and practices explored throughout *A Spirituality of Fundraising* are relevant in all cultures.

I invite you into my friendship with Henri and encourage you to trust him as your guide. The workbook that follows Henri's text is designed to help you undertake what Henri has called a "personal spiritual workout." It involves engaging the ancient spiritual disciplines of listening, journaling, and prayer and then developing action steps. You may be tempted to bypass this way of being present to Henri's teaching, but, in so doing, you risk truncating the crucial process of allowing Henri's voice to descend into your heart so that his words become part of you, part of your story. There are two ways to read this workbook: quickly or methodically and prayerfully. Nothing will change if you quickly read this book and then set it aside.

Many years ago, when Henri first spoke the words you soon will read, his fundraising vision was unknown and untested beyond his personal experiences. Today, Henri's vision and text have spread across the world. You have the benefit of knowing that Henri's vision has empowered tens of thousands of people. You can trust that it will be fruitful for you too.

To live fruitful lives. Is that not what we most desire? To love and be loved. To be a source of blessing in the world and to contribute to the well-being of others. To be part of a community in which we can give and receive. To be faithful to God and to be God-like in how we live our lives. Henri sees fundraising as a task and a process that will help you to live a deeply fruitful life. Like an artist who paints or an author who writes, the fundraiser engages in a creative process that brings beauty into the world. I've experienced beauty in asking people what they really care about and listening deeply. I also know the beauty of sharing my story and the story of the people with whom I stand and asking someone to become a financial partner in L'Arche's work.

Fundraising has taken me to the center of my heart and to the heart of things that are truly important in life. May it continue to do so—both for me and for you.

—Nathan Ball, February 2019

HOW TO USE THIS WORKBOOK

This workbook contains the entire text of *A Spirituality of Fundraising* by Henri J. M. Nouwen, along with a four-week study guide to help you develop your own spirituality of fundraising, using Henri's and my guidance. Each week contains five short sessions that will take around 15–20 minutes to complete. On days one through four of each week, I invite you to listen and journal. You will need a separate journal for your writing. Day five's session concludes with a time of prayer and action steps. At the end of each week, I've included touchstones. Thus, each week will include the following:

- **Listen.** After you have read the material for each day, spend 5–10 minutes listening. Become quiet. Simply sit and notice your feelings and thoughts. What is the text saying to you? What is your strongest feeling? What do you "hear"?
- **Journal.** Write down the feelings and insights that emerged from your listening practice. Use the journaling prompts to write or make notes about specific aspects of the text.
- **Pray.** Take time with what you've heard and journaled throughout the week, offering it to God and asking for guidance. This section will include a written prayer that you can use to get started. Prayer is not only about what you say; it is about sitting in God's presence and making yourself available to that presence.
- **Act.** Healthy spirituality always invites and pushes us past our comfort zones. The spiritual practice of embracing disruption is about naming the discomfort and pushing past it by committing to act in specific ways. This is about putting theory into practice through action. Some action steps will be suggested.

- **Touchstone.** These short, personal affirmations are designed to draw you forward into the beliefs, commitments, and practices that will enable you to engage fundraising as a spiritual practice. They also serve as a reminder for what you have read and learned over the past week. I encourage you to copy the ones that inspire you most into your journal and refer to them often.

Using the Workbook as an Individual

- **Read.** Each of the four weeks has an introduction followed by five short daily reflections. Allow yourself the time and space to read each daily reflection. Don't rush.
- **Reflect.** Each day, after reading the reflection, take time to listen and journal, using the prompts.
- **Pray.** On the last day of each week, take time to pray and reflect.
- **Act.** Follow the prompts for action. Your inner work must express itself through public engagement. Contemplation flows into action. Take the risk to implement your action steps. Break through your resistance. Do the work.

Using the Workbook with a Group

- **Prepare.** You may want to meet with your group for five sessions. The first session would be introductory, and a leader (if there is one) can lay out the structure of the group for the following four weeks. Each participant should work through the week's work prior to that week's session, that is, complete week 1 before the group meeting about week 1.
- **Pray.** Begin with two minutes of silence. Then, two participants will read the prayer or poem for the week slowly, one after the other.
- **Share.** Each person may take two minutes to share an insight or inner movement that was important in his or her personal study from the preceding week. Receive what each person says without comments, questions, or dialogue. Take personal notes as people speak. Learn from one another.
- **Discuss.** Dialogue and engage one another. Follow up on the sharing or use the suggested questions as discussion prompts.

- **Give thanks.** End your session by inviting each group member to express a word of gratitude. Each person can finish this sentence: "Right now, I'm grateful for . . . ." Your gratitude might be for an idea, a feeling, an insight, or for the people in your group.

Establishing Your Intention

Like many people, each year I have an annual physical. My physician checks me out in a variety of ways and helps me to refocus on my health for the coming year. I usually leave the appointment grateful for a renewed sense of purpose and direction regarding my health. But several years ago, about eighteen months after my family had moved from Toronto to St. Louis, this did not happen.

I was not long into the examination when my new physician asked, "Are you exercising regularly, three or four times each week?"

"Quite often," I responded. (Lie. I had basically stopped.)

We chatted a little more and he said, "You've gained fifteen pounds in the past eighteen months. Has your diet changed?" I quickly replied that I almost had decided to become a vegetarian and that I never go to fast food restaurants. (Lie. Over the past year I had been eating far too many unhealthy snacks and was feeling guilty about this new habit.) As the appointment ended, my doctor asked how things were going at home and at work. I said things were pretty good. My family's recent move had been stressful, but I explained that I was grateful in many ways.

"I'm still adjusting to our new home, but life is good." (Another lie. Parenting was unusually stressful. My wife and I were going through a difficult time. I felt unmotivated and discouraged in my work, which had led to significant self-doubt. In short, I was a mess!) Six months later, after continuing to struggle in a similar fashion, I went back to see my physician. I told him that I had not been honest at my last appointment and asked if I could have a do-over. "Of course," he said, "but let me ask you a question. What do you want? What is your intention? Because unless you're clear about that, it will be hard for you to make good choices." We had a great conversation, and I left feeling supported in my renewed commitment to take care of myself in a holistic way.

I was struck by the fact that my doctor did not ask me why I had not been honest. He didn't try to guilt trip me. Neither did he advise me to set goals, find a therapist, or stop eating junk food (all of which are good ideas). Rather, by asking about my intention, he invited me to consider my well-being not just with my head but with my heart and to pay attention to my desire to be healthy and whole. He invited me to think about the kind of life I wanted (healthy or unhealthy) and the hope I had for the future.

Embarking Upon a Journey

With Henri and me as your guides, you are embarking upon a journey to embrace fundraising as a Spirit-filled opportunity to build friendships and community around a shared vision. Fundraising will take you deep inside yourself, where you will encounter beliefs, feelings, attitudes, and behaviors that will be simultaneously wonderful and terrible. The journey of fundraising will also take you into the world where you will be called to engage with others in ways that may be uncomfortable. But this engagement also may be a source of deep blessing for you and for others. Henri invites you to travel to a new place in your relationship with money and fundraising. Therefore, a mindset of trust, curiosity, and adventure is imperative. Like any other important journey, how you prepare will affect the quality of your experience.

Clarity of mind and heart about why you want to make this journey will help you to persist when the going gets tough. Henri's text will likely inspire and empower you. Perhaps you will find yourself excited about fundraising after reading it. That's wonderful! Though fundraising is not for the faint of heart, you will be surprised by the gifts and blessings that fundraising can bring into your life and the life of your community. Getting there may take time, but you can and will reach your destination. Please trust this.

The journey begins by establishing your intention. Ask yourself, *Why do I want to learn more about fundraising? What do I want to achieve through studying Henri's book and using this workbook? Who or what is calling me to deepen my understanding of fundraising? Am I prepared to do the inner work that is needed, or am I merely a curious observer? Am I ready to explore the idea of fundraising as ministry?* A clear intention will guide your attitude and choices along the way. An example of an intention is this: *I intend to open myself fully to fundraising as a positive, life-giving activity that will bring me closer to God and to others.* Or this: *I intend to move from fear to love and trust around fundraising.* There are no "right" answers here. This is the time to announce your fundraising intention to yourself—and perhaps to others—by writing it down. Doing this will create an inner readiness to learn and grow. If you wake up tomorrow and want to revise your intention, do so.

Once you have established your intention, I invite you to look inside yourself and be truthful about where you are right now. In other words, create an honest starting place. Be generous and forgiving with yourself. Acknowledge any tensions you experience concerning fundraising—the tension between asking for money and your understanding of the spiritual life; the tension between your longing for more freedom in your relationship with money and the way that money controls your life; the tension between your desire to do your job well and the ambivalence you feel about the project, community, or organization that has asked you to raise money; the tension between your need for money and your resistance to asking for it. Along with any tensions, recognize what brings you excitement and passion about being part of a community, project, or ministry that can only be possible because ordinary people will invest their money with trust and generosity.

Reading with Your Heart

Much of reading is acquisitive; you want to learn how to do something or to gain knowledge, so you pick up a book on a particular topic and look for the information you need. This book asks something different of you. Henri always wrote from his heart with the hope that his readers would read with their hearts and, in so doing, begin to see and experience life in new ways. "Spiritual reading," Henri wrote, "is reading with an inner attentiveness to the movement of God's Spirit in our outer and inner lives. With that attentiveness, we will allow God to read us and to explain to us what we are truly about."[1] Henri invites you to allow his words to descend into your heart and sow themselves in the innermost core of your being.

As you approach *A Spirituality of Fundraising*, allow yourself at least ninety minutes to read the text slowly from beginning to end. Highlight, mark, sketch, doodle, scribble, and write all over this book. Notice your feelings as much as your thoughts. Linger over the words; contemplate and absorb them. Don't rush. Stop often, especially when you read a phrase or a sentence that touches you. Acknowledge the excitement, joy, surprise, or anxiety that you feel. Don't allow yourself to get stuck in your head. There is nothing to memorize. There is no test. Your only task is to engage the ideas with openness and curiosity and see what parts of Henri's spiritual vision for fundraising find fertile ground in your heart.

It's time to begin! I suggest that you take a deep breath and choose an attitude of gratitude. You may not have imagined that the task of fundraising would take you into a deeper relationship with yourself and God. Trust that a modest investment of time to explore and develop your own approach to fundraising will be good for you and for others. You are embarking on a beautiful, Spirit-filled journey. Be grateful that you have Henri as your trustworthy guide. Give thanks for who you are, and embrace this journey in a wholehearted way.

A SPIRITUALITY OF FUNDRAISING[1]

Henri J. M. Nouwen

Preface

Speaking one day to a large audience gathered to hear about fundraising as ministry, Henri Nouwen learned that the booksellers in the lobby had sold all their copies of his latest book. At noon, he set out for the nearest bookstore to purchase more copies for them to have on hand. En route to his car, he was approached by a casually dressed young man who requested money to get home in France. Characteristically, Henri said, "Jump into the car and come with me. Tell me about yourself."

As they drove along, the young man explained his unsuccessful attempt to secure a hoped-for position in Canada and his inability to get to his home because of lack of funds. Return ticket in hand, he was leaving that evening for Paris but had no money to get from there to his hometown in the south of France. When Henri had completed his purchase, returned to the conference center, and as they were parting, Henri gave the young man two hundred dollars and asked him to send news upon his safe arrival home.

Later that day, following his lectures and just before leaving, the booksellers in the lobby handed Henri an envelope in gratitude for his kindness to them. Opening the card, Henri found a thank-you note and a check for two hundred dollars!

Generosity begets generosity. This is especially so when generosity is rooted in the rich soil of relatedness. Henri, because of his open and Spirit-filled attitude, always sought points of relatedness with the people he met. Henri's generosity with money grew from a larger generosity of self. His desire for authentic relationships stirred this desire in others, and so he experienced people as generous with their time, their concern, and also their money.

In many ways, Henri was a rich and generous man with the means and the openness to give. He also needed funds to support his many passionate interests. So he experienced fundraising from both sides, and his vision of it arose from his actual experience of being asked to donate money and of asking others to support his various ministries. Then, with time, his vision extended beyond the personal to the universal.

Like many of us, Henri's vision began with the notion of fundraising "as a necessary but unpleasant activity to support spiritual things." But his passion for ministry and for living from a spiritual motivation led him further and deeper until he could finally say with conviction, "Fundraising is first and foremost a form of ministry."

In this short talk Henri is on fire and passionate about God's kingdom. He offers all those motivated by the Spirit of God a new set of glasses to see and live their fundraising ministry as integral to their mission: "Fundraising is as spiritual as giving a sermon, entering a time of prayer, visiting the sick, or feeding the hungry!"

As ministry, fundraising includes proclamation and invitation as well as conversion. "Fundraising is proclaiming what we believe in such a way that we offer other people an opportunity to participate with us in our vision and mission." For Henri, the proclamation and invitation involve a challenging call to conversion for fundraisers and donors alike. "Fundraising is always a call to conversion." All are called into a new, more spiritual relationship with their needs and their resources. Henri encourages fundraisers to become more confident and joyful, standing up in their asking without apology. And in this vision they do not profit alone, because donors also participate in a new communion with others while becoming part of a much larger spiritual vision and fruitfulness.

Because of the fruitful relationship between the Henri Nouwen Society and Upper Room Ministries, this project and its passage from idea to reality authenticate the manuscript's spiritual message about ministry, vision, asking, giving, and receiving. I believe and trust that the collective investment of so many people in creating this book will be multiplied many times through its impact on the fundraising vision and practice of countless individuals and organizations.

—Sue Mosteller, CSJ
The Henri Nouwen Legacy Trust

Acknowledgements

On September 16, 1992, Henri Nouwen spoke to the Marguerite Bourgeoys Family Service Foundation about fundraising. It was an informal address that came from the heart without need of a written manuscript. Happily, the talk was recorded on tape and the transcript lightly edited. From time to time copies of the talk were given to individuals or organizations involved in fundraising ventures. The positive response to the fresh vision of fundraising that Henri was beginning to articulate led Sue Mosteller, Henri's literary executrix, to consider ways of distributing the piece more widely.

The manuscript was given as a gift to the fledgling Henri Nouwen Society for its own work in financial development. In April 2003, I was contacted about the possibility of preparing Henri's text for publication. The call from the Nouwen Society was inspired by my relationship with Henri. During my doctoral studies at Yale University I served for five years as Henri's teaching, research, and editorial assistant. He was my mentor and friend. *Weavings*, the journal I edited for twenty-four years, still seeks to reflect in its own time and place the spiritual vision that Henri so beautifully embodied.

I have exercised the liberty that Henri regularly granted me to add material where his ideas invited expansion or his transitions needed elaboration. Labors of love attract community, and this project has confirmed that truth. Nathan Ball and Sue Mosteller from the Nouwen Legacy Trust have been deeply involved in all aspects of the work. Despite a ferocious schedule, Sue even found time to write the Preface. Wendy Greer and Robert Durback generously offered suggestions for the margin excerpts from Henri's other writings. Resa Pearson, Elaine Go, and Sue Smith of Pearson & Company created a design as appealing and accessible as Henri's life and faith. Pamela Hawkins reviewed the manuscript with an editor's careful eye. And Robin Pippin of Upper Room Books guided the whole process with gentle skill. Finally, I would like to thank you, the reader, for taking up Henri's vision of fundraising as ministry and carrying it forward in ways he could hardly have imagined.

—John S. Mogabgab
Upper Room Ministries

Fundraising is a subject we seldom think about from a spiritual perspective. We may think of fundraising as a necessary but unpleasant activity to support spiritual things. Or we might believe that fundraising reflects a failure to plan well or to trust enough that God will provide for all our needs. Indeed, quite often fundraising is a response to a crisis. Suddenly our organization or faith community does not have enough money, so we begin to say: "How are we going to get the money we need? We have to start asking for it." Then we realize that we are not used to doing this. We may feel awkward and a little embarrassed about it. We begin to worry and wonder: "Who will give us money? How will we ask them?"

Fundraising as Ministry

> Ministry is, first of all, receiving God's blessing from those to whom we minister. What is this blessing? It is a glimpse of the face of God.
>
> —*Here and Now*

From the perspective of the gospel, fundraising is not a response to a crisis. Fundraising is, first and foremost, a form of ministry. It is a way of announcing our vision and inviting other people into our mission. Vision and mission are so central to the life of God's people that without vision we perish and without mission we lose our way (see Proverbs 29:18; 2 Kings 21:1-9). Vision brings together needs and resources to meet those needs (see Acts 9:1-19). Vision also shows us new directions and opportunities for our mission (see Acts 16:9-10). Vision gives us courage to speak when we might want to remain silent (see Acts 18:9).

Fundraising is proclaiming what we believe in such a way that we offer other people an opportunity to participate with us in our vision and mission. Fundraising is precisely the opposite of begging. When we seek to raise funds we are not saying, "Please, could you help us out because lately it's been hard." Rather, we are declaring, "We have a vision that is amazing and exciting. We are inviting you to invest yourself through the resources that God has given you—your energy, your prayers, and your money—in this work to which God has called us." Our invitation is clear and confident because we trust that our vision and mission are like "trees planted by streams of water, which yield their fruit in its season, and their leaves do not wither" (Ps. 1:3).

Fundraising is also always a call to conversion. And this call comes to both those who seek funds and those who have funds. Whether we are asking for money or giving money we are drawn together by God, who is about to do a new thing through our collaboration (see Isaiah 43:19). To be converted means to experience a deep shift in how we see and think and act. To be converted is to be clothed in our right mind, to come to ourselves the way the younger son did when he was starving far from his true home (see Luke 15:14-20). It is a shift of attention in which we set our mind on divine things (see Matthew 16:23). "Do not be conformed to this world, but be transformed by the renewing of your minds, so that you may discern what is the will of God—what is good and acceptable and perfect" (Rom. 12:2). Fundraising as ministry involves a real conversion.

In fundraising, people who work in the marketplace are often wiser than people who work in the church. Those who are involved in big business know that you never get much money if you beg for it. I remember visiting a successful fundraiser in Texas whose office was filled with beautiful things. I said, "How do you dare to ask for money in this office?" He replied, "My office is part of my way of approaching people. It is meant to communicate that I know how to work with money, that I know how to make money grow. This inspires confidence in the people I meet that their investment will be well used."

This approach is not for everyone, and being surrounded by nice things is not the right motivation for fundraising as ministry. Important here is that spiritually this man was saying, "I ask for money standing up, not bowing down, because I believe in what I am about. I believe that I have something important to offer." Without apology he invites people to be a part of his vision.

In fundraising as ministry, we are inviting people into a new way of relating to their resources. By giving people a spiritual vision, we want them to experience that they will in fact benefit by making their resources available to us. We truly believe that if their gift is good only for us who receive, it is not fundraising in the spiritual sense. Fundraising from the point of view of the gospel says to people: "I will take your money and invest it in this vision only if it is good for your spiritual journey, only if it is good for your spiritual health." In other words, we are calling them to an experience of conversion: "You won't become poorer, you will become richer by giving." We can confidently declare with the Apostle Paul: "You will be enriched in every way for your great generosity" (2 Cor. 9:11).

If this confident approach and invitation are lacking, then we are disconnected from our vision and have lost the direction of our mission. We also will be cut off from our donors, because we will find ourselves begging for money and they will find themselves merely handing us a check. No real connection has been created because we have not asked them to come and be with us. We have not given them an opportunity to participate in the spirit of what we are about. We may have completed a successful transaction, but we have not initiated a successful relationship.

Here we see that if fundraising as ministry invites those with money to a new relationship with their wealth, it also calls us to be converted in relation to our needs. If we come back from asking someone for money and we feel exhausted and somehow tainted by unspiritual activity, there is something wrong. We must not let ourselves be tricked into thinking that fundraising is only a secular activity. As a form of ministry, fundraising is as spiritual as giving a sermon, entering a time of prayer, visiting the sick, or feeding the hungry. So fundraising has to help us with our conversion too. Are we willing to be converted from our fear of asking, our anxiety about being rejected or feeling humiliated, our depression when someone says, "No, I'm not going to get involved in your project"? When we have gained the freedom to ask without fear, to love fundraising as a form of ministry, then fundraising will be good for our spiritual life.

When those with money and those who need money share a mission, we see a central sign of new life in the Spirit of Christ. We belong together in our work because Jesus has brought us together, and our fruitfulness depends on staying connected with him. Jesus tells us: "I am the vine, you are the branches. Those who abide in me and I in them bear much fruit, because apart from me you can do nothing" (John 15:5). With him, we can do anything because we know that God surrounds us with an abundance of blessings. Therefore, those who need money and those who can give money meet on the common ground of God's love. "God is able to provide you with every blessing in abundance, so that by always having enough of everything, you may share abundantly in every good work" (2 Cor. 9:8). When this happens, we can indeed say with Paul, "There is a new creation!" (2 Cor. 5:17). Where there is a new creation in Christ, there the kingdom of God is made manifest to the world.

Helping the Kingdom Come About

> To set our hearts on the kingdom therefore means to make the life of the Spirit within and among us the center of all we think, say, or do.
>
> —*Making All Things New*

Fundraising is a very concrete way to help the kingdom of God come about. What is the kingdom? Jesus is clear that if we make the kingdom our first priority, "all these other things will be given you as well" (Matt. 6:33, NJB). The kingdom is where God provides for all that we need. It is the realm of sufficiency where we are no longer pulled here and there by anxiety about having enough. "So do not worry about tomorrow: tomorrow will take care of itself" (Matt. 6:34, NJB). Jesus also compares the kingdom to a mustard seed, "which, at the time of its sowing, is the smallest of all the seeds on earth. Yet once it is sown it grows into the biggest shrub of them all and puts out big branches so that the birds of the air can shelter in its shade" (Mark 4:31-32, NJB). Even a seemingly small act of generosity can grow into something far beyond what we could ever ask or imagine (see Ephesians 3:20)—the creation of a community of love in this world, and beyond this world, because wherever love grows, it is stronger than death (see 1 Corinthians 13:8). So when we give ourselves to planting and nurturing love here on earth, our efforts will reach out beyond our own chronological existence. Indeed, if we raise funds for the creation of a community of love, we are helping God build the kingdom. We are doing exactly what we are supposed to do as Christians. Paul is clear about this: "Make love your aim" (1 Cor. 14:1, NJB).

Our Security Base

> The converted person knows himself or herself and all the world in God.
>
> —*¡Gracias!*

Those of us who ask for money need to look carefully at ourselves. The question is not how to get money. Rather, the question is about our relationship with money. We will never be able to ask for money if we do not know how we ourselves relate to money.

What is the place of money in our lives? The importance of money is so tied up with relationships that it seems almost impossible to think about it without also thinking about how family life has influenced our relationship with money.

How many of us know how much money our father or mother earns, or has, at the moment? Do we normally talk with them about their money? Is money ever the subject of dinner table conversation? Are family conversations about money usually anxious, angry, hopeful, satisfied? Did our parents talk with us about money when we were children? Do they talk with us about it now? Did they teach us skills in how to handle money? And in our own turn, do we discuss our financial affairs with our children? Are we comfortable telling them how we earn it and how we use it?

Money is a central reality of family relationships. It is also a central reality in our relationships with people, institutions, and causes beyond family life. Therefore we need also to think about this side of our financial life.

How do we spend the money we have? Are we inclined to save it so we will be prepared for emergencies, or do we spend it because we might not have it later? Do we like to give our money to friends, to charities, to churches, to political parties, to educational institutions? Where are we, in fact, giving our money? Are we concerned about whether our gift is tax deductible? Does that question even occur to us?

How would we feel if people used the money we gave them in ways other than those for which we gave it? Imagine giving a thousand dollars to someone thinking the money would be used to help needy children. Later it becomes clear that this person used the donation for a trip to the Caribbean. Would we get angry? Once a seminary president said to me, "If you never want to be fooled, you will never give money."

If money touches our relationships with family members as well as the world beyond our home, it also reaches into our inner life. It is interesting that the phrase "personal worth" can mean both the extent of our financial assets and our value as a human being. Once again, some questions may help us explore this aspect of our relationship with money.

How does having, or not having, money affect our self-esteem, our sense of value? Do we feel good about ourselves when we have a lot of money? If we do not have much money, do we feel bad about ourselves? Is a low or even modest income a source of embarrassment? Or do we think money doesn't matter at all?

Money and power go together. There is also a real relationship between power and a sense of self-worth. Do we ever use money to control people or events? In other words, do we use our money to make things happen the way we want them to happen? Do we ever use money simply to give others the freedom to do what they want to do? How do we feel when people ask us for money?

If any of these questions makes us uncomfortable, it may be because talking about money is one of the greatest taboos around. Money conversations are a greater taboo than conversations about sex or religion. People may say, "Don't talk about religion, that's my private business." Others may say, "Don't talk about sex, it belongs in the bedroom." Discussing money is even harder for many people. And this becomes immediately noticeable when we must do some fundraising. Often we do not feel that asking for money is an easy thing to be "up front" about.

The reason for the taboo is that money has something to do with that intimate place in our heart where we need security, and we do not want to reveal our need or give away our security to someone who, maybe only accidentally, might betray us. Many voices around and within us warn us of the danger of dependence. We fear being dependent on others because of the idea that dependence is a threat to our security.

A friend once told me how often his father would say, "Son, be sure you don't become dependent on anybody. Be sure you do not have to beg for what you need. Be sure that you always have enough money so you can have your own house, your own things, and your own people to help you. As long as you have some money in the bank, nothing bad can really happen to you."

The pressure in our culture to secure our own future and to control our lives as much as possible does not find support in the Bible. Jesus knows our need for security. He is concerned that because security is such a deep human need, we do not misplace our trust in things or people that cannot offer us real security. "Do not store up treasures for yourselves on earth, where moth and woodworm destroy them and thieves can break in and steal. But store up treasures for yourselves in heaven, where neither moth nor woodworm destroys them and thieves cannot break in and steal. For wherever your treasure is, there will your heart be too" (Matt. 6:19-21, NJB). We cannot find security if our heart is divided. So Jesus says something very radical: "No servant can be the slave of two masters: he will either hate the first and love the second, or be attached to the first and despise the second. You cannot be the slave both of God and of money" (Luke 16:13, NJB).

What is our security base? God or mammon? That is what Jesus would ask. He says that we cannot put our security in God and also in money. We have to make a choice. Jesus counsels: "Put your security in God." We have to make a choice whether we want to belong to the world or to God. Our trust, our basic trust, Jesus teaches, has to be in God. As long as our real trust is in money, we cannot be true members of the kingdom.

All those questions I asked were simply to help us consider whether we are, perhaps, still putting our security in money. "Those who trust in their riches will wither, but the righteous will flourish like green leaves" (Prov. 11:28). What is the true base of our security?

People Who Are Rich

> You are sent into this world to believe in yourself as God's chosen one and then to help your brothers and sisters know that they also are beloved sons and daughters of God who belong together.
>
> —*Finding My Way Home*

The Bible is unambiguous about God's concern for the poor. "Since there will never cease to be some in need on the earth, I therefore command you, 'Open your hand to the poor and needy neighbor in your land'" (Deut. 15:11; see Isaiah 58:6-12). From its birth the church has recognized the privileged place of the poor in God's sight. "Listen, my beloved brothers and sisters. Has not God chosen the poor in the world to be rich in faith and to be heirs of the kingdom that he has promised to those who love him?" (James 2:5). Indeed, the poor and suffering remind us that the Son of God became poor for our sake (see 2 Corinthians 8:9). God loves the poor, and so do those who follow Christ. In loving and serving the poor, we have the beautiful opportunity to love and serve Jesus. "In truth I tell you," Jesus says to his disciples, "in so far as you did this to one of the least of these brothers of mine, you did it to me" (Matt. 25:40, NJB).

But sometimes our concern for the poor may carry with it a prejudice against the rich. We may feel that they are not as good as the poor. I remember hearing a professor at a theological school say about a large, wealthy church: "This cannot be an authentic church." Perhaps we think the rich have more money than they deserve, or that they got their wealth at the expense of the poor. Maybe we find it hard to love the rich as much as the poor. But nobody says we should love the rich less than we love the poor. The poor are indeed held in the heart of God. We need to remember that the rich are held there too. I have met a number of wealthy people over the years. More and more, my experience is that rich people are also poor, but in other ways.

Many rich people are very lonely. Many struggle with a sense of being used. Others suffer from feelings of rejection or depression. It may seem strange to say, but the rich need a lot of attention and care. This is very important to recognize, because so often I have come in touch with rich people who are totally in the prison of thinking, "The only thing people see in me is money. Wherever I go, I am the rich aunt or the rich friend or the rich person, so I stay in my little circle, because as soon as I leave it people say, 'She's rich!'"

Once a woman came to see me. She was very wealthy and very depressed. She had been from one psychiatrist to another and had paid them huge fees with few results. She said, "You know, Henri, everybody is after my money. I was born into wealth and my family is wealthy. That's part of who I am, but that's not all there is. I am so afraid that I am loved only because of my money and not because of who I really am."

Some years ago a person who had read a number of my books called my assistant at the university where I was teaching. He said, "I'm reading Henri Nouwen's books, and I wonder, does he need any money? I really want him to write more, and it is expensive to write books these days." I was away for four months, so my assistant called me and said, "There is a banker here who wants to help you with money." I did not know what to do, so I said, "Well, go and have dinner with him." So they went out for dinner and then continued to have dinner every week. They talked about all sorts of things and by the time I returned to the university, the two had become good friends.

I joined my assistant for dinner with the banker, who said, "Henri, I know you don't know a thing about money." I said, "How do you know?" He answered, "I know people like writers don't know a thing about money." What he was really saying, however, was, "What you are writing about is something I want to talk with you about on a more personal level than I can by just reading your books. I believe that the only way I can develop a personal relationship with you is through my strength, which is being a banker." Ultimately, this man was saying, "I need something that I think you have, and I really would like to get to know you." I replied, "Let's not talk about money right now. Let's just talk about you."

Over time we became close friends. Year after year he would give me a few thousand dollars. I used the money well and told him what I had done with his gift. But the money was not the most important part of our relationship. Most important was that he was able to share who he was and I was able to do the same in an atmosphere of mutual respect and trust.

When my friend died his family said to me, "We would like to continue supporting you because of the love that you had for our husband and our father. We want you always to feel that there are people who will support you because we love you, as our husband and father loved you."

Through the poverty of the rich man something very much of the kingdom developed. The money was real, but it was not the most impressive part of our relationship. We all had resources: mine were spiritual and theirs were material. What was impressive was that we all wanted to work for the kingdom, to build a community of love, to let something happen that was greater than we were individually.

My banker friend helped me see that we must minister to the rich from our own place of wealth—the spiritual wealth we have inherited as brothers and sisters of Jesus Christ. In him "all the jewels of wisdom and knowledge are hidden" (Col. 2:3, NJB). We must have the courage to go to the rich and say, "I love you, and it is not because of your money but because of who you are." We must claim the confidence to go to a wealthy person knowing that he or she is just as poor and in need of love as we are. Can we discover the poor in this person? That is so important because it is precisely in this person's poverty that we discover his or her blessing. Jesus said, "How blessed are you who are poor" (Luke 6:20, NJB). The rich are also poor. So if we ask for money from people who have money, we have to love them deeply. We do not need to worry about the money. Rather, we need to worry about whether, through the invitation we offer them and the relationship we develop with them, they will come closer to God.

Asking

> Take away the many fears, suspicions, and doubts by which I prevent you from being my Lord, and give me the courage and freedom to appear naked and vulnerable in the light of your presence, confident in your unfathomable mercy.
>
> *—A Cry for Mercy*

If our security is totally in God, then we are free to ask for money. Only when we are free from money can we ask freely for others to give it. This is the conversion to which fundraising as ministry calls us. Already we have seen that many people have a hard time asking for money because money is a taboo subject. It is a taboo subject because our own insecurities are connected with it, and so we are not free. We also are not free if we are jealous of the rich and envy their money. And we are not free if we feel anger toward those who have money, saying to ourselves, "I'm not so sure that they made all that money in an honest way." When rich people make us jealous or angry, we reveal that money in some way is still our master and that therefore we are not ready to ask for it.

I am deeply concerned that we do not ask for money out of anger or jealousy, especially when these feelings are well hidden behind polite words and a careful presentation of our request for funds. No matter how polished our approach is, when our asking comes from anger or jealousy we are not giving the person the means to become a brother or sister. Rather, we put the person in a defensive position because he or she realizes that there is some kind of competition going on. The offer to participate in our vision and mission is no longer for the kingdom. It no longer speaks in the name of God, in whom alone our security is secure.

Once we are prayerfully committed to placing our whole trust in God and have become clear that we are concerned only for the kingdom; once we have learned to love the rich for who they are rather than what they have; and once we believe that we have something of great value to give them, then we will have no trouble at all in asking someone for a large sum of money. We are free to ask for whatever we need with the confidence that we will get it. That is what the gospel says: "Ask, and it will be given to you; . . . knock, and the door will be opened to you" (Matt. 7:7, NJB). If for some reason a person says "No," we are free to respond gratefully. We can trust that the Spirit of Christ who is guiding us is also guiding that person. Perhaps her financial resources are more urgently needed elsewhere. Maybe he is not yet ready to make a real commitment. Perhaps we need to listen more deeply to the Spirit so that our asking will be clearer and our vision more attractive. Because we approach potential donors in the Spirit of Christ, when we ask them for money we can do so with an attitude and in an atmosphere of confident freedom. "Christ set us free, so that we should remain free" (Gal. 5:1, NJB).

Asking people for money is giving them the opportunity to put their resources at the disposal of the kingdom. To raise funds is to offer people the chance to invest what they have in the work of God. Whether they have much or little is not as important as the possibility of making their money available to God. When Jesus fed five thousand people with only five loaves of bread and two fish, he was showing us how God's love can multiply the effects of our generosity (see Matthew 14:13-21). God's kingdom is the place of abundance where every generous act overflows its original bounds and becomes part of the unbounded grace of God at work in the world (see 2 Corinthians 9:10-15).

A New Communion

> Community is the fruit of our capacity to make the interests of others more important than our own.
>
> —*Bread for the Journey*

When we ask people for money to strengthen or expand the work of the kingdom, we are also inviting them into a new spiritual communion. This is very important. In Paul's letter to the Romans we read: "We are well aware that the whole creation, until this time, has been groaning in labour pains. And not only that: we too, who have the first-fruits of the Spirit, even we are groaning inside ourselves, waiting with eagerness for our bodies to be set free" (Rom. 8:22-23,

NJB). This groaning comes from deep within us, and indeed from within all creation. It is the sound of our yearning for communion with God and with one another, a communion that transcends the limitations of time and space.

At the same time, this groaning also expresses God's passionate yearning for communion with us and with all that God created. God desires "that the whole creation itself might be freed from its slavery to corruption and brought into the same glorious freedom as the children of God" (Rom. 8:21, NJB). This is the freedom of true spiritual communion. Asking for money is a way to call people into this communion with us. It is saying, "We want you to get to know us." Gathered together by our common yearning, we begin to know this communion as we move together toward our vision.

How does spiritual communion manifest itself concretely? When fundraising as ministry calls people together in communion with God and with one another, it must hold out the real possibility of friendship and community. People have such a need for friendship and for community that fundraising has to be community-building. I wonder how many churches and charitable organizations realize that community is one of the greatest gifts they have to offer. If we ask for money, it means that we offer a new fellowship, a new brotherhood, a new sisterhood, a new way of belonging. We have something to offer—friendship, prayer, peace, love, fidelity, affection, ministry with those in need—and these things are so valuable that people are willing to make their resources available to sustain them. Fundraising must always aim to create new, lasting relationships. I know people whose lives center around the friendship they find in churches, monasteries, service organizations, and intentional Christian communities. These people visit or volunteer, and it is in these settings that they find nurture and support. If these people have money, they will give it; but that is not the point. When compared with new freedom and new friends in a new communion, the money is the least interesting thing.

Spiritual communion also reveals itself in a new fruitfulness. Here the radical nature of fundraising as ministry becomes clear. In the world, those who raise funds must show potential donors a strategic plan that convinces donors their money will help to increase the productivity and success of the organization. In the new communion, productivity and success may also grow as a result of fundraising. But they are only by-products of a deeper creative energy, the energy of love planted and nurtured in the lives of people in and through our relationship with Jesus. With the right environment and patient care, these seeds can yield a great harvest, "thirty and sixty and a hundredfold" (Mark 4:20). Every time we approach people for money, we must be sure that we are inviting them into this vision of fruitfulness and into a vision that is fruitful. We want them to join us so that together we begin to see what God means when God says, "Be fruitful" (Gen. 1:28).

Finally, I would like to return to the relationship between money and we who seek it through fundraising. Just as the work of building the community of love asks us to be converted in our attitude toward money, so also this same activity invites each of us to greater faithfulness to our personal call, our unique vocation. Our own call must be deepened and strengthened as a result of our fundraising. Sometimes this brings us right to the heart of our struggle with our vocation. During my own fundraising work, people have said to me: "I will give you money if you will take up the challenge to be a better pastor, if you will stop being so busy and be more faithful to your vocation. You run around and talk your head off, but you don't write enough. I know that this is difficult for you—to shut the door and sit behind your desk and not speak to anyone, but I hope that my contribution will support you in your writing." This is part of the fruitfulness of the community of love. By calling us to deeper commitment to our particular ministry, fundraising helps to make visible the kingdom that is already among us.

Prayer and Gratitude

> The Spirit reveals that we belong not to a world of success, fame, or power but to God.
>
> —*Bread for the Journey*

How do we become people whose security base is God and God alone? How can we stand confidently with rich and poor alike on the common ground of God's love? How can we ask for money without pleading, and call people to a new communion without coercing? How can we express not only in our way of speaking but also in our way of being with others the joy, vitality, and promise of our mission and vision? In short, how do we move from perceiving fundraising as an unpleasant but unavoidable activity to recognizing fundraising as a life-giving, hope-filled expression of ministry?

Prayer is the spiritual discipline through which our mind and heart are converted from hostility or suspicion to hospitality toward people who have money. Gratitude is the sign that this conversion is spreading into all aspects of our life. From beginning to end, fundraising as ministry is grounded in prayer and undertaken in gratitude.

Prayer is the radical starting point of fundraising because in prayer we slowly experience a reorientation of all our thoughts and feelings about ourselves and others. To pray is to desire to know more fully the truth that sets us free (see John 8:32). Prayer uncovers the hidden motives and unacknowledged wounds that shape our relationships. Prayer allows us to see ourselves and others as God sees us. Prayer is radical because it uncovers the deepest roots of our identity in God. In prayer we seek God's voice and allow God's word to penetrate our fear and resistance so that we can begin to hear what God wants us to know. And what God wants us to know is that before we think or do or accomplish anything, before we have much money or little money, the deepest truth of our human identity is this: "You are my beloved son. You are my beloved daughter. With you I am well pleased" (see Luke 3:22). When we can claim this truth as true for us, then we also see that it is true for all other people. God is well pleased with us, and so we are free to approach all people, the rich or the poor, in the freedom of God's love. Whether people respond to our fundraising appeal with a "Yes," a "No," or a "Maybe" is less important than the knowledge that we all are gathered as one on the holy ground of God's generous disposition toward us. In prayer, therefore, we learn to trust that God can work fruitfully through us no matter where we are or who we are with.

As our prayer deepens into a constant awareness of God's goodness, the spirit of gratitude grows within us. Gratitude flows from the recognition that who we are and what we have are gifts to be received and shared. Gratitude releases us from the bonds of obligation and prepares us to offer ourselves freely and fully for the work of the kingdom. When we approach fundraising in a spirit of gratitude, we do so knowing that God has already given us what we most need for life in abundance. Therefore our confidence in our mission and vision, and our freedom to love the person to whom we are talking about donating money, do not depend on how that person responds. In this way, gratitude allows us to approach a fundraising meeting without grasping neediness and to leave it without resentment or dejection. Coming and going, we can remain secure in God's love with our hearts set joyfully on the kingdom.

Your Kingdom Come

> The mystery of ministry is that we have been chosen to make our own limited and very conditional love the gateway for the unlimited and unconditional love of God. Therefore, true ministry must be mutual.

> —*In the Name of Jesus*

Fundraising is a very rich and beautiful activity. It is a confident, joyful, and hope-filled expression of ministry. In ministering to each other, each from the riches that he or she possesses, we work together for the full coming of God's kingdom.

Listen

Sit silently for five to ten minutes, and listen for what the text has stirred within your heart. What parts of the reading stand out to you? What energized you? What challenged you?

Journal

1. What excites you about Henri's vision? Write a short letter to Henri, expressing your hopes and expectations.

2. What makes you anxious about or fearful of fundraising?

3. Who will support and encourage you on your fundraising journey?

From the perspective of the gospel, fundraising is . . . first and foremost, a form of ministry.

—A Spirituality of Fundraising

Week One Goal

To explore the concept of fundraising as ministry and develop a personal understanding of how fundraising can become an integral part of your spiritual journey

Most of us only think about fundraising when we are approached to give financially or when we are asked to help raise money to support a community, organization, or cause. Given that well over 1.5 million registered nonprofit organizations exist in the United States alone, according to the National Center for Charitable Statistics, we all most likely have been asked to participate financially in one or more faith community or organization. But for those of us for whom fundraising is part of our responsibility in a paid or volunteer position, we have to think about fundraising more often. And when we do, it's not usually from a spiritual perspective.

Fundraising involves money, and many of us can't understand how money and spirituality could mix. Jesus teaches that "it is easier for a camel to go through the eye of a needle than for someone who is rich to enter the kingdom of God" (Matt. 19:24), which suggests that money (and, by implication, fundraising) is a spiritual roadblock.

We tend to see fundraising as part of the material, market economy in which we are all buying and selling and making deals. Fundraising is the necessary, unpleasant work of finding the money to keep things going. The building needs to be built, salaries paid, and programs executed. Fundraising is what we do to "keep the lights on." This feels far from the more "spiritual" work of loving and of integrating our lives into an ever-deepening experience of purpose, meaning, and transcendence. Henri turns this way of thinking upside down by asserting with confidence and passion that fundraising is a beautiful, necessary, and powerful manifestation of love that propels us on a path that can be spiritually transformational for everyone involved—all while bringing forth the financial resources needed in any given situation.

Ministry

Every person has the ability to be a minister. We all are called to make love our aim and to bear witness to the power of love in the world. Ministry isn't only work for "professionals"—that is, pastors, church employees, missionaries, or those who give their lives to serve the least among us. Ministry is the unique way each of us uses our gifts and our energy to share God's love with the world. This ministerial work can be done at home, at work, or in the marketplace. But before we can do the work of ministry, we first must affirm our identity as ministers, as people who have accepted the call to be servants of love, each in our unique way. Fundraising is one such form of ministry.

In choosing to see fundraising as a form of ministry, we affirm our identities as servant leaders. We are servants first; service is the lens through which we fundraise and lead. Our disposition toward potential donors is one of service. We are serving our community and its mission and needs. As fundraisers, we are also in a privileged position to encourage people to give generously. The fundraiser as servant strives to be free and open-hearted. This means, for example, celebrating a donor's choice to give a gift that is not directed toward us or our cause—even when we would have been grateful to see the gift come to our mission.

The fundraiser as servant is a countercultural notion. In a world that values money more than everything else, it is a short jump to say that if we make more money, give more money, or raise more money, then we are more valuable and have more power. Servant fundraisers—or servant fundraising boards or committees—recognize this illusion and make decisions to counteract it. Fundraising may be a mission-critical role for a faith community or organization, but it is not more important than any other role.

Holding the Paradox

The fundraiser as minister must learn the art of holding paradox. Our work is urgent, yet it needs time to unfold. On one hand, the people and mission we serve cannot thrive—or even survive—without money. The task of fundraising is both important and pressing. Often people's lives depend upon the work we do. It is right and essential that we should have goals and objectives and that we remain accountable to others to maintain momentum in our fundraising work because, like any task or vocation, fundraising requires discipline.

On the other hand, we are called to take the long view. The fundraiser as minister places his or her trust not in himself or herself but in the infinitely larger power of love. We must have faith in ourselves, knowing that each of us can make a difference. But we also are one small part of the magnificent story that has unfolded before us and will continue long after we are gone. It takes real emotional maturity and understanding to hold onto this paradox.

The Fundraiser's Prayer

In 1979, inspired by the life of the San Salvador priest Oscar Romero, Father Kenneth Untener, a priest from Michigan, wrote a homily that included a poetic reflection. A copy of his short reflection hangs on the wall above my desk. It is sometimes called "The Romero Prayer," but I call it "The Fundraiser's Prayer." Even though the author never uses the words *fundraising* or *money*, the prayer beautifully captures the paradox that is intrinsic to the vision of fundraising as ministry. This will be our prayer for week one.

Prophets of a Future Not Our Own[1]

It helps, now and then, to step back and take a long view.

The kingdom is not only beyond our efforts, it is even beyond our vision.

We accomplish in our lifetime only a fraction of the magnificent enterprise that is God's work. Nothing we do is complete, which is a way of saying that the Kingdom always lies beyond us.

No statement says all that could be said.

No prayer fully expresses our faith.

No confession brings perfection.

No pastoral visit brings wholeness.

No program accomplishes the Church's mission.

No set of goals and objectives includes everything.

This is what we are about.

We plant the seeds that one day will grow.

We water the seeds already planted, knowing that they hold future promise.

We lay foundations that will need further development.

We provide yeast that produces far beyond our capabilities.

We cannot do everything, and there is a sense of liberation in realizing that.

This enables us to do something, and to do it very well.

It may be incomplete, but it is a beginning, a step along the way, an opportunity for the Lord's grace to enter and do the rest.

We may never see the end results, but that is the difference between the master builder and the worker.

We are workers, not master builders; ministers, not messiahs.

We are prophets of a future not our own.

DAY ONE: LOVE

When we give ourselves to planting and nurturing love here on earth, our efforts will reach out beyond our own chronological existence. Indeed, if we raise funds for the creation of a community of love, we are helping [build the reign of God].

—*A Spirituality of Fundraising*

T oday, we begin with one of life's toughest questions: *What is my deepest desire?* No person or community, creed or contract can answer this question for us. With his eye on the life and teachings of Jesus, Henri suggests that our deepest desire be to help create a community of love in the world. Our mission, our overarching purpose, is to love. There are many ways to make this purpose concrete in our lives. We may be surprised (and excited!) to read Henri's assurance that fundraising is a practical and privileged way to build a community of love, bring justice into the world, and learn how to walk humbly with God. Fundraising is a way of loving deeply.

> What is important is how well we love. God will make our love fruitful, whether we see that fruitfulness or not.
>
> —*Bread for the Journey*

So why are we interested in or engaged in fundraising? Because no one else will get involved? Because of a sense of obligation? Because we were elected to a fundraising committee? Henri invites us to join him in reimagining fundraising by announcing to the universe that our deepest desire is to be people who love deeply and who see fundraising as a way of living out that purpose and mission.

Jesus calls us to love—the gritty, unsentimental kind that he lived and taught. This kind of love fulfills our deep human need to bring hope, justice, wholeness, and healing into the world. Henri writes beautifully about the fruits of loving deeply:

> Do not hesitate to love and to love deeply. . . . The wider your inner community becomes, the more easily you will recognize your own brothers and sisters in the strangers around you. . . . As you love deeply the ground of your heart will be broken more and more, but you will rejoice in the abundance of the fruit it will bear.[2]

Recently, I was on a plane, and, as often happens, the man beside me asked, "What kind of work do you do?"

Feeling mischievous, I answered, "I have devoted my life to creating a community of love."

The man took another look at me, paused, and decided to continue. "Well, what kind of community, and what specifically do you do?" We had a great conversation!

Listen

Sit silently for five to ten minutes, and listen for what today's reading has stirred within your heart. What energized you? What challenged you?

Journal

1. Write about your desire to be a person who loves deeply. How do you keep your desire alive? How do you align your choices and behavior with your desire?

2. How do you view fundraising? How can fundraising, as Henri suggests, be a way of loving?

DAY TWO: BEING LOVED

What God wants us to know is that before we think or do or accomplish anything, before we have much money or little money, the deepest truth of our human identity is this: "You are my beloved son. You are my beloved daughter. With you I am well pleased."

—A Spirituality of Fundraising

Some readers may be asking themselves, *Why are we still talking about love? I want to learn about fundraising.* One of the fundamental tenets of the spiritual life is that *being* comes before *doing*. As fundraisers, we must take care of the *being* part of our lives. This means knowing who we are, knowing our value—no matter what we achieve or don't achieve. It means having clear values and increasing our self-awareness as we engage people from various walks of life. The journey of fundraising holds unique challenges, and we easily can stumble along the path or get discouraged if we are not grounded in our *being*—that is, who we most deeply are.

In the meditation from day one, we affirmed our deep desire to be women and men of love and to do our part to create a community of love. Loving others (*doing*) is often easier than allowing ourselves to be loved (*being*). Henri insists that in order to act lovingly and to embrace fundraising as a way of loving, we must allow ourselves to be possessed by God's love. To grow in the knowledge and experience of God's love is to know who we are and where we belong. Everything we say or do as fundraisers will be determined by the depth of our experience of love and by our ability to return to God's loving embrace.

In his extensive writing, Henri uses tens of thousands of words to help us understand how our entire lives depend upon our relationship with God. He refers to God as "the One," "the Divine Lover," "Divine Love," "Lord of the Universe," "the True Source," "Unchanging Love," "Compassionate Creator," "Companioning Presence," "Giver of Life and Breath," "the Divine Comforter," "the Holy One," and "the Great Awakener." This God, the One who has a thousand names, is the One in whom we live and love and have our being.

Henri's names for God may spark something inside of us or give us new ways of addressing the immense Love in our lives. We also may use different names for God; even so, we can resonate with Henri's description of living a conscious spiritual life:

> I don't often "feel" like a beloved child of God. But I *know* that that is my most primal identity and I *know* that I must choose it above and beyond my hesitations. Strong emotions, self-rejection, and even self-hatred justifiably toss you about, but you are free to respond as you will. You are not what others, or even you, think about yourself. You are *not* what you do. You are *not* what you have. You are a full member of the human family, having been known before you were conceived and molded in your mother's womb. . . . As a spiritual practice claim and reclaim your primal identity as a beloved daughter or son of a personal Creator.[3]

Nothing is more important to fundraising as ministry than the choice to claim and reclaim our eternal belovedness. It is our anchor.

Listen

Sit silently for five to ten minutes, and listen for what today's reading has stirred within your heart. What energized you? What challenged you?

Journal

1. How might a more profound experience of your own belovedness impact your fundraising work?

2. How might you connect more deeply to your experience of belonging to God?

DAY THREE: A CALL TO CONVERSION

Fundraising is also always a call to conversion. And this call comes to both those who seek funds and those who have funds. . . . To be converted means to experience a deep shift in how we see and think and act.

—A Spirituality of Fundraising

If fundraising as ministry is about loving and being loved, then it is also a call to conversion for everyone involved. First, rooted in our call to help build a community of love, we are challenged to shift from an ashamed stance of bowing down as we ask for money to standing confidently. Fundraising is not begging. Our culture wants us to judge ourselves and others in terms of status, money, and power. We "look up" to some people and "look down" upon others. When we are fully grounded in love, nobody is beneath us and nobody is above us. It takes courage to develop this confidence in who we are and apply this to our work as fundraisers.

Second, we are called to be converted in relation to our needs. "I can't ask people for money unless I know they will say yes," some fundraisers say. But fundraising as ministry calls us to be converted from our fear of rejection. We needn't be depressed or feel humiliation if someone says no to our invitation to share his or her time, interest, and money. Our self-worth needn't depend on external forces or on the commitments or the whims of

---

The converted person sees, hears, and understands with a divine eye, a divine ear, a divine heart.

—Show Me the Way

---

others. Instead, our internal belief in who we are and our belovedness will sustain us in the face of rejection.

Third, we are called to shift our perspective from a singular focus on financial needs and goals to a more integrated effort that includes—and even prioritizes—the quality of the spiritual journey of everyone involved. This is radically counter-cultural. The world wants us to believe that money is the most important part of life. Because we often find ourselves believing this lie, we are anxious about and preoccupied with money—earning it, investing it, saving it, spending it, asking for it, and giving it. Fundraising as ministry calls us to shift our focus away from money so that we can be present to potential financial partners as people who have needs and desires and who want to express their values through philan-thropy in meaningful ways. This shift in perspective calls us to view our need for money as a community or an organization as less important than the spiritual well-being of our potential financial partners.

Fourth, as askers and givers, our conversion asks that we do the work of identifying what we have learned about money. Our core orientations toward money, security, spending and saving, giving and asking, and wealth and poverty have been passed down to us by others and taught by our surrounding culture. The "story" that we tell about money in our lives and in the world needs to be examined and altered in light of the values we hold—values such as love, justice, community, solidarity, and courage. Fundraising as ministry is not business as usual when it comes to the role of money in our lives.

Fifth, all involved in the process of asking and giving are called to conversion in the way that we relate to our resources. National and global economic injus-tice is a fact, one that many of us have a hard time facing. Privileges afforded to some are not granted to all. My resources—financial and otherwise—are not primarily a result of hard work or God's blessing. I had no (or very little) con-trol over many aspects of my life that have gotten me to where I am today—the moment in history when I was born, the family or culture into which I was born, my core gifts and personal qualities, the random kindnesses that have impacted my life, the teachers who have shaped me. My life is rooted in gift. Everything we have is a gift. We are called to integrate this truth into how we relate to our resources and how we give, share, and invest in others.

Finally, Henri insisted that fundraising is a communal process. The conversion here is from "me" to "we," from "them" to "us." Fundraising as ministry is not the activity of one or two gifted people. It is not about getting the right volunteer or the most talented paid fundraiser who will get the financial resources we need. Henri once wrote, "The spiritual life is a treacherous undertaking that we best not attempt alone."[4] He could just as easily have said the same about fundraising. We need to be converted from the thinking that raising money is somebody else's business. Instead, we should think about how each of us can contribute to the process of raising funds.

Anyone on a conscious spiritual journey knows that conversion is an ongoing process. Sometimes this conversion entails jolts of awareness about what we need to change in our attitudes and lives. At other times, it's only when we slow down and take time to listen to our own hearts and to others that we gradually become aware of the call to change. Either way, we are called to embrace the process of conversion.

Listen

Sit silently for five to ten minutes, and listen for what today's reading has stirred within your heart. What energized you? What challenged you?

Journal

1. Whether you are new to fundraising or a seasoned professional, think of a moment when you encountered internal hesitation or fear when asking for money. What did you fear, and how might you transform your fear into a call to conversion?

2. As you read and reflect on the vision of fundraising as ministry, where are you experiencing the call to conversion? Where are you being challenged to make a radical shift in how you see, think, and act?

DAY FOUR: THE BLESSING

Those who need money and those who can give money meet on the common ground of God's love.

—*A Spirituality of Fundraising*

We are all blessed simply to exist, and we are all called to be a blessing for others. But when we consider the word *blessing*, we usually think of what we say before a meal, the good things we receive in life, or the words at the end of a church service or wedding. Henri invites us to shift our understanding of the word *blessing* from a noun to a verb. To bless others, we must allow love to flow out of our lives and into the lives of others and into our communities. This flow of love allows us and others to recognize and acknowledge God's presence in our lives, both in weakness and in strength, in times of plenty and in times of poverty.

As ministry, fundraising is equally concerned about the well-being of the asker, the giver, and the beneficiaries. Each part of this fundraising equation can be a blessing to the other parts. If the process of asking, giving, and receiving does not lift and honor each party, then it is not ministry and service. It goes without saying that fundraising as ministry can never be about the subtle manipulation, even with the best of intentions, of people's thoughts or emotions so that they will write a check. Fundraising as ministry expects that we will engage, dialogue, dream, and pray together. In so doing, we all can benefit spiritually.

I often find myself doubting the power of fundraising as ministry. I ask myself, *Will the process of inviting people into partnership through a financial gift really bring them into an experience of relational richness? Can I bless them with my request?* I've discovered that the only way to know is to ask. Often, after asking someone for a gift, no matter the response, I will say something like this: "Thank you for who you are and for our conversation. It is a blessing for me to be part of this process with you. I know our discussion has been good for the mission of my organization. I'd love to check in with you. Has this process been good for you?"

My question is not about seeking personal reassurance. When I reach out to someone with a request for partnership, I hope that my asking can bless him or her as well. Fundraisers who see themselves as ministers create spaces for people to experience life as a blessing.

Listen

Sit silently for five to ten minutes, and listen for what today's reading has stirred within your heart. What energized you? What challenged you?

———

Too many fundraisers do not believe in the possibility of fundraising being a blessing for themselves and for others. The quality of relationships for all involved is always more important than short-term and long-term monetary results.

We can use many tools and metrics to evaluate the effectiveness of our fundraising. They help us to stay focused on the process of engaging people in our cause or mission, but they also may inadvertently reduce fundraising to a process of finding cash for a mission instead an opportunity to bless all involved.

———

Journal

1. Describe an occasion when someone invited you to make a commitment of some kind, to be of service, to give money, or to take on a responsibility that eventually blessed you. How was that experience meaningful to you?

2. What does an invitation suggest about the relationship between you and the person doing the inviting (for example, trust, appreciation, welcome, friendship)?

DAY FIVE: TAKING STOCK

As a form of ministry, fundraising is as spiritual as giving a sermon, entering a time of prayer, visiting the sick, or feeding the hungry.

—A Spirituality of Fundraising

Some time ago, at a L'Arche event, a mutual friend introduced me to a successful entrepreneur. I was somewhat taken aback when his first words to me were, "So you're the one with the sticky fingers." This interaction was a good reminder that not everyone views fundraising through the lens of ministry. Nevertheless, I smiled and reached out to shake his hand.

"Don't worry," I replied. "My hands aren't sticky! What I really do in my work is talk to people about what is important to them and how they are working to realize those priorities. Sometimes that leads to conversations about L'Arche, and sometimes it doesn't. Either way, I love the dialogue."

Perhaps this entrepreneur viewed fundraising through a lens of business development, sales, or marketing. While none of these lenses excludes the notion of fundraising as ministry, choosing ministry as our primary lens for viewing fundraising has important implications. First, we must remember that love is our aim. Our fundraising must be rooted in an understanding of love: We are born in love; we are born to love; and fundraising is a way of loving. As we begin to engage in fundraising as ministry, Henri insists that we develop the spiritual practice of embracing our belovedness and acknowledging the belovedness of others.

Second, fundraising as ministry joyfully embraces the journey of conversion. Both asking for money and giving money invite us to change how we see, think, and act. This does not happen automatically. The fundraiser as minister knows that darkness resides in each of us, in our communities, and in our culture; however, he or she chooses to nurture an attitude of humility.

Third, fundraising as ministry carries with it the hope and desire that everyone involved be lifted up. Each person blesses and is blessed. The process of asking, giving, and receiving money is about bringing healing and wholeness into the world.

Finally, fundraising as ministry is a communal task. The financial needs and aspirations of a community or an organization must be discerned collectively and then acted upon in a way that involves more people than a single paid or volunteer fundraiser or a standalone committee. All leaders in an organization, whatever their responsibility, play an important part in creating a culture of generosity. Their roles include both affirming the act of fundraising as ministry and engaging the process personally. If this does not happen in a significant way, then the financial results will always be mediocre, and the mission will suffer accordingly.

We must remember that, ultimately, fundraising as ministry both is and is not about money. As in other areas of our lives, the way to hold the paradox is not by trying to resolve it but through the development of spiritual detachment. This is about letting go. Directly and respectfully asking people for money is an important, sacred, mission-critical task. We engage in this task with joy, giving thanks for the opportunity to participate in ministry in this way. And, yes, it matters to us and to others that we get the money that we need. At the same time, we are called to "let go" of this monetary result. Why? So that we can remain free and trusting and stay focused on the quality of the relationship with the giver. Spiritual detachment is the lifelong process of learning how to open our hands, minds, and hearts.

Let me be clear: Fundraising as ministry does not mean that money is unimportant. It does not mean that we ask for less money or that we make fewer monetary requests. It is not about conflating fundraising with counseling or pastoral care. It does mean that we place the highest value on relationships—not money. It means that we want the asking and giving of fundraising to be done in freedom. Fundraising as ministry is open and transparent.

Henri has made the case that fundraising is a credible spiritual path. The choice to follow that path with all its twists and turns is yours and mine. Whatever our choice, the world urgently needs women and men, professionals and volunteers, and people from every culture to embrace fundraising as a way of participating in the reign of God. It's about love and justice. It's about you and me.

Pray

Reread "The Fundraiser's Prayer" on page 42. Your life is a gift, and you are a gift to others. Think about prayer as an opportunity to commune with God and to be present to the desires of your heart.

Act

1. Identify someone who is actively involved in the fundraising process: a volunteer, a pastor, a donor, or a paid fundraiser. Invite this person to coffee or lunch to discuss the idea of fundraising as ministry. (The hardest part of this action may be taking the risk to make the invitation. Getting out of your comfort zone is a huge part of fundraising.)

2. Look back at your journal entry from day three and the actions you have hesitated to take in fundraising. Pick one and map out a plan for how you will take this action in the next week to ten days. (After you have done this, return to your journal and write about how you felt after completing the action and what you learned about yourself and fundraising along the way.)

Week One Touchstones

1. I recognize the work of fundraising as a spiritual practice.

2. I confidently invite others to become financial partners because I believe deeply in the mission I represent and the change I want to make in the world.

3. I believe that asking a potential financial partner for a gift to support the mission to which I have been called is an act of ministry.

4. I remind myself that asking for money is part of a larger collective work of creating an extensive and inclusive community of love and justice.

5. I know myself to be a beloved child of God. When I forget, I have practices to bring me back to this truth such as prayer, journaling, and confiding in a friend.

6. I care deeply about the people whom I ask for money. I only want them to participate financially if they feel called to do so and will be blessed by their giving.

What is our security base? God or mammon? That is what Jesus would ask. He says that we cannot put our security in God and also in money. We have to make a choice.

—*A Spirituality of Fundraising*

Henri writes that if we place our security completely in God, then we will discover we are free from what has hindered us from asking others for money. But what does it mean to place our security totally and fully in God? And what would such security entail? Would it include physical safety? Or social, psychological, and financial security? Unfortunately, putting our security in God does not mean that we will be safe from illness, job loss, violence, poverty, or divorce. It does not mean that our community or organization will get all the money it thinks it needs. Ironically, in spite of our many efforts to "secure" our lives, we often feel insecure and afraid. We live in a world where danger and uncertainty abound.

Week Two Goal

To explore the meaning that money has for you and the roots and structure of your relationship with money

Henri asks us to acknowledge that we look to the wrong sources for our security, significance, and belonging. Ultimate security will not be found through having a life partner, nor will it come through children. It will not be found in the work that we do, in the mission we embrace, or in the size of our retirement account. We are called to recognize our attachment to the world of money and possessions as a primary method of coping with the insecurity in our lives. But material possessions cannot give long-lasting security. In fact, the opposite is true. We need to detach from our possessions.

There is a voice in all of us that says, *If only I had enough money—or more money—I would feel fully secure and happier.* Of course, money is important. But behind this need lurks the seductive voice that tells us that life would be better with more money. Sometimes this voice is that of simple greed, especially when we know that one of the biggest injustices in the world is that so many people do not have enough money to secure their basic needs.

All major religious traditions, including Christianity, teach that security is an illusion and that insecurity is a way of life. We cannot banish insecurity from our lives. What, then, does it mean to put our trust in God? It is about listening to our soul and trusting that we can and will find that sacred place deep inside ourselves where we know that we are loved and that we are precious. In this place, fear no longer governs our actions, and we know that we belong. God offers us the security of love—out of which we were created, live, and have our being—and God asks us to return to this love again and again, whenever we find ourselves afraid and placing our trust in things of this world.

One of the main themes of Henri's book *The Return of the Prodigal Son* is that our spiritual work is to "return." A modern retelling of Jesus' famous parable goes something like this: The younger of two sons asks his parents for his share of the family inheritance. His parents, though concerned by his request, agree. The son leaves home with his money, which he proceeds to squander quickly. Eventually, he finds himself broke and homeless. Embarrassed and ashamed, he decides to return home. Upon his return, his parents welcome him with open arms and throw a big party to celebrate. The older brother, who had quietly witnessed his brother's departure and return, goes to his parents and expresses his deep resentment of his irresponsible brother. The older brother points out his own faithfulness in staying home to help run the family business. The parents explain how much they love their older son but that they cannot support his resentment. The parents' hearts are filled with joy because the son that they thought they had lost has come home.

We can see ourselves as the younger child in our need to return to the place of belonging within God's expansive family. Equally, we can see ourselves as the elder child who also needs to return to the Source of Life. Whether we find ourselves resonating more with the younger child or the older child, we all need to return to God as our security base, gently refocusing ourselves, letting go of those people, things, or ideas in which we have placed our trust, and choosing our relationship with God as the place of our ultimate security. Like the tide that rolls in and out, we constantly move among life's shadows, glimpsing the light, sometimes feeling its warmth as it pierces the darkness. We come, and we go. We are lost, and we are found. We leave, and we return.

The call to conversion, to go back to our true place of belonging, means gently returning to the heart of God and giving thanks for the gift of life and our unique presence in the world. Henri describes it this way: "Jesus' whole life and preaching had only one aim: to reveal this inexhaustible, unlimited motherly and fatherly love of his God and to show the way to let that love guide every part of our daily lives."[1]

The following poem is attributed to the thirteenth-century poet Rumi. It will be our prayer for week two.

> Come, come, whoever you are.
> Wanderer, worshipper, lover of living, it doesn't matter
> Ours is not a caravan of despair.
> Come even if you have broken your vows a thousand times,
> Come, yet again, come, come.

DAY ONE: UNDERSTANDING OUR RELATIONSHIP WITH MONEY

The question is not how to get money. Rather, the question is about our relationship with money. We will never be able to ask for money if we do not know how we ourselves relate to money.

—*A Spirituality of Fundraising*

What is the place of money in our lives?" Henri asks us. To answer this question, we must first examine our personal experiences with money from childhood to now. When I was a child, I had friends whose families were "worth" a lot. My family was not "worth" very much. As an adolescent, I remember dutifully spending $100 of my hard-earned money to buy large quantities of food essentials for my parents—cooking oil, potatoes, and rice. As the oldest child, I felt a responsibility to help my parents care for our family. This experience, for example, plays a role in my relationship to money. Others may have similar stories to mine, while others' experiences may differ greatly. Even so, no matter what we were taught about money by our family of origin or what we believe because of what our culture teaches us, one thing is universally true: Our relationship with money is complex and can bring out the best and the worst in us.

Money impacts all our relationships and can be the cause of tension, anger, and resentment within families and couples. Almost nothing absorbs more of our time and attention than money, yet most people's relationship with money goes unspoken and unexplored throughout their lives. Most of us did not learn how to talk about money—even with those closest to us. Our joys, and struggles related to money are mostly hidden. Because our relationship to money is so complex and resides in an intimate place inside us, we don't open ourselves easily to others to let them know how money affects our lives—how we spend it, how we save it, how it causes us anxiety or creates resentment within relationships. Talking honestly about money is so tough that Henri says people find it more taboo than speaking honestly about religion or sex.

Whether we are asking or giving, the fundraising process is a perfect opportunity to examine our relationship with money. This examination may be difficult, but it will benefit us, those we love, and our larger communities in ways that go far beyond our interest in fundraising

Listen

Sit silently for five to ten minutes, and listen for what today's reading has stirred within your heart. What energized you? What challenged you?

Journal

1. Henri invites you to explore your relationship with money by creating a money autobiography. Do this in your fundraising journal. I encourage you to spend as much time as possible with the questions from Henri's text. Nothing will help you understand your relationship to money better than writing a money autobiography. Go to the section titled "Our Security Base" in Henri's text on pages 27–29. Choose two or three questions under each of the following categories, and write your answers:
   - Family life

   - People, causes, and institutions

- My inner life

- My sense of self-worth

2. Why does talking about money and your relationship with money feel taboo or off-limits?

DAY TWO: MONEY AND POWER

Money and power go together. . . . Do we ever use money to control people or events? . . . Do we ever use money simply to give others the freedom to do what they want to do?

—*A Spirituality of Fundraising*

Talking about power is essential in our work to build a more just world. We must consider not only the link between money and power but also the relationship between power and gender, power and race, power and religion, power and politics, and power and technology. Given the huge role that power plays in our world, it is surprising that we don't talk about it more frequently. When we do talk about power, it is often about the misuse and abuse of power, the multiple ways in which power, concentrated among the few and not spread among the many, is used to diminish rather than to build up humanity. The gospel critique of power is that it is often used against—instead of for—those who are the weakest and most vulnerable among us.

In terms of fundraising, Henri asks us to reflect honestly on the link we see between power and money in our relationships and in our philanthropy. How do we use the "money power" that we have? Do we cling to this power, hoarding it for ourselves, our families, or our friends, or do we use our power in the spirit of service to others and for justice? How does having or not having money affect our sense of personal value? How does it affect our sense of personal power? And how does money affect the value we place on others?

To consider these questions on a deeper level, we also may want to consider how we define power. Is power something that comes primarily from material possessions and wealth? How can power come from inside ourselves? What if we imagine power not as something that a person possesses but as the energy between people as they share the gifts, resources, and wisdom to which they have access? From this perspective, the power of a community is not found in the number of buildings it owns or the size of its bank account but in the quality of friendship and trust among its members.

We all need money, desire money, and use money in multiple ways. Whether we are asking for, giving, or receiving money, the money–power dynamic is always present. Too often it is the "elephant" in the room that we don't talk about. But we must acknowledge the power dynamic that is connected to money and choose to clothe ourselves in a spirit of service. We must seek to diminish the ways in which we use money to control people or situations. The inner, spiritual movement of fundraising as ministry calls us to accept—not deny—the power dynamic between money and power and to do the important work of putting that power into service for others.

Listen

Sit silently for five to ten minutes, and listen for what today's reading has stirred within your heart. What energized you? What challenged you?

Journal

1. Answer the following questions in your fundraising journal: How do I experience my own desires for money and for power through money? How do I use the "money power" that I have? Do I cling to this power, or do I use power in the spirit of service and for justice?

2. How often do you seek money or power as a form of personal security? What might change if you begin to reimagine power as the shared gifts and resources within a community of people?

DAY THREE: LIVING WHOLEHEARTEDLY

We have to make a choice whether we want to belong to the world
or to God.

—A Spirituality of Fundraising

Some people have told me they believe Henri is a saint. By using that term, I think they mean that he was especially close to God and helped others know and trust the Spirit of Truth. Personally, I am cautious about trying to figure out who is or who isn't a saint, and I am drawn to the idea that perhaps "the least of these" (Matt. 25:40) among us are the true saints. Still, if Henri is a saint, it would be because he engaged life in a deeply trusting and wholehearted manner. He remained curious about everyone and everything. He loved to listen to people, and he saw listening from the heart as a precious act of love, a powerful way of affirming the beauty of each person's life. He knew that listening is how we let people know that they matter. (This is a central reason why listening is such an important skill for fundraisers.)

Henri loved the creativity and dynamism of life. He wanted to be fully engaged in the world's accomplishments and brokenness, its loveliness and its pain. He was fascinated by the many ways people live in the world. He enjoyed talking to and learning from entrepreneurs and business people, educators and artists, construction workers and mail carriers. He befriended people whether young or old. He knew writers, pastors, teachers, plumbers, doctors, and politicians. He had a radical conviction that each person is at the same time gifted and disabled, strong and weak.

In the context of Henri's rich life experience, some readers may be surprised to know that he struggled with a profound inner restlessness about which he spoke and wrote with enormous honesty. Despite his many friends and the admiration he received for his work as a pastor, teacher, and writer, he often felt alone and unloved in the world. This pain was never far from him. Yet he chose to believe that his life was one small but important part of a much bigger story, a story of divine love that had meaning and purpose. He chose, again and again, to let go of the kinds of attachment to people, reputation, and emotions that would keep him from trusting God more deeply. He learned to love the world around him and to release the illusion that anything outside of him would satisfy his deepest needs for security and belonging.

For me, Henri is a saint not because he lived a better life than you or I but because he placed his trust in God amid adversity. His agony produced an inner, emotional darkness that threatened his well-being. He struggled with voices that told him he was not lovable. Henri modeled how we can choose to trust the small, quiet voice of Love within that says, *You are my beloved.* Henri needed people and community to help him hear that voice. He was disciplined in creating space each day when he could pray in solitude and with others. He read scripture and sacred texts through which he could hear the voice of Love. He found safe relationships in which he could express his anguish when it overwhelmed him and receive the support he needed.

Wholehearted living does not mean the absence of struggle. It means that we know what it's like to have our hearts filled with love, and we do everything we can to return to that place of inner wholeness. The inner, spiritual work of fundraising calls us to become women and men who are wholehearted. We are community builders who model the quality of life and love in which we invite others to invest. Here are four practices that can help us live wholeheartedly:

- **Keep the faith.** Life is more than what we can see around us. In so many ways, our lives are a mystery to us. When we resist the temptation to try and understand everything (an impossible feat), we choose to trust that God is alive and at work in the world. Even though our beliefs and understanding may change over time, let us "keep the faith" in God's loving presence.
- **Give money generously.** A couple recently said to me, "Financial giving is one of our highest values. We are committed to practicing radical generosity." As fundraisers, whether our income is small or large, giving away more money

than we think we can is a response to the needs of the world. This type of giving will help us to deepen our trust in God. Let's consider this question honestly: How much money is enough for me and my family? Once we decide on a figure, we can ask ourselves what it would look like to give the rest away.

- **Join or create a conversation about faith and money.** Disconnecting from the lure of money, possessions, and our egos can only become a spiritual practice if it is done with others. Who will support us as we examine the relationships among faith, justice, and money? Wholeheartedness requires conscious resistance to things that take up the wrong kind of space in our hearts.

- **Commit to wholeheartedness.** Most of us want to give and receive love and to experience joy and peace. We want to get along with people and to be patient and generous. We hope to have adventure, quality relationships, and lots of laughter in our lives. None of these things can be purchased. Once we have created a personal picture of what wholeheartedness means for us, we can commit to that vision. When we stray from our vision, we can return to God as the place of our security and the source of love that will fill our heart.

Every time I take a step in the direction of generosity, I know that I am moving from fear to love.

—*The Return of the Prodigal Son*

Listen

Sit silently for five to ten minutes, and listen for what today's reading has stirred within your heart. What energized you? What challenged you?

Journal

1. What gets in the way of living wholeheartedly? When have you struggled to keep your faith alive? Describe what was happening in your life at that time.

2. Reflect on your giving practices. Do you give as much as you'd like? If not, what's stopping you? What's enough for you and your family?

DAY FOUR: FINANCIALLY RICH AND POOR DESERVE LOVE

The poor are indeed held in the heart of God. We need to remember that the rich are held there too.

—A Spirituality of Fundraising

We all have moments when we do not treat others as if they are of equal value, deserving of love, and held in the heart of God. This is commonly called the "value-action gap"—that is, the space between our values or beliefs and our actions. When we blame and shame people, we cannot simultaneously affirm their belovedness. Our value-action gaps are often related to the degree in which our sense of security lies externally—in money, status, possessions, and so on. The more we look outside our heart and soul for ultimate security, the harder embracing the intrinsic belovedness of every person will be for us.

In week one, we discussed how viewing fundraising as ministry calls us to the conversion and transformation of our deep beliefs about and actions toward people who are different from us. We often mistrust people whose ways are different from ours. And these different people may be as close to us as family members or as (seemingly) distant as people of different ethnicities, religious practices, or socioeconomic classes. When it comes to money, some of us, for a variety of reasons, tend to have a prejudice against people who are economically poor. Others tend to have a prejudice against those who are wealthy. Our judgments can be explicit and harsh, or they can simmer just below the surface. Regardless, Henri calls us to act out of the following truths:

- Both the financially poor and financially wealthy are held in the heart of God.
- No matter our access to money, we are all poor, vulnerable, and disabled in various ways.
- Every person has unique gifts and resources to share with the world.
- Money should never be the most important part of any relationship.
- If we ask people for money, then we also must love them and only ask if we sense that our invitation will be good for them spiritually.

Active, engaged fundraising is about reaching out to others, listening to their stories, and sharing ours. It is about loving people deeply with a love that does not depend upon filiation or familiarity and expects nothing in return. Welcoming the stranger, whether she be rich or poor, is not a straightforward path. It's a journey to be embraced. Fundraising takes us to the heart of that journey.

Listen

Sit silently for five to ten minutes, and listen for what today's reading has stirred within your heart. What energized you? What challenged you?

Journal

1. Who do you tend to exclude or have difficulty embracing because they are different? What makes their life experiences different from yours? Write about this person or group of people, and imagine yourself in their shoes. How can you shift your attitude toward them?

2. Reflect on your feelings about people who are wealthy. How do you perceive them? Are you drawn to them? envious of them? Do you judge them? What stories do you tell yourself about people who are rich? Ask yourself the same questions about people who are poor.

DAY FIVE: TAKING STOCK

Jesus knows our need for security. He is concerned that because security is such a deep human need, we do not misplace our trust in things or people that cannot offer us real security.

—A Spirituality of Fundraising

Take a deep breath. Let's remind ourselves that the question of where to place our security is not one to be solved but to be lived. There is nothing outside of us that will give us the security we need and want. "Life is precious," Henri once wrote, "Not because it is unchangeable, like a diamond, but because it is vulnerable, like a little bird. To love life means to love its vulnerability, asking for care, attention, guidance, and support. Life and death are connected by vulnerability."[2] Our need for security means that we are vulnerable. How we live with this vulnerability significantly defines our lives.

The problem for most of us is that we don't fully believe that vulnerability is precious because we are afraid of it. From an early age, we discover that relationships are difficult to navigate and that life can be very painful. We learn to be careful when it comes to matters of the heart, and we become masters in disguising our true feelings and building walls around our heart. We work hard to diminish our feelings of insecurity by placing our trust in money, reputation, achievement, and relationships. None of these is inherently bad. These are the primary ways through which we express who we are and find meaning and purpose. But none of them will bring us the deep, lasting security and peace for which we long.

Jean Vanier spoke often about the reality of our vulnerability and lack of security by saying that our lives are bookended by two cries: the cry of the utterly dependent, vulnerable newborn and the cry that comes in the last season of our lives, in the weakness of our aging and dying. We are vulnerable at the beginning of our lives, at the end of our lives, and during our in-between years. It is who we are. But how do we embrace our vulnerability and our need for security? Fundraising as ministry reminds us to approach raising money with a deep respect for the universal human experience of vulnerability and the universal human need for security. Fundraising as ministry invites us to explore these aspects of life honestly and to have the courage to invite others to do the same. We display integrity as fundraisers by inviting others to give as we also are giving. We invite others to place their security more deeply in God as we are doing the same. Wrestling with humanity's vulnerability, need for security, and desire for money is not just for philosophers and theologians. It is an important and urgent matter for each of us and takes us right to the center of our vision of fundraising as ministry.

Pray

End this week with a short time of stillness, using the Rumi prayer-poem with which you began this section. May you always find the courage and the humility to return to God "a thousand times."

> Come, come, whoever you are.
> Wanderer, worshipper, lover of living, it doesn't matter
> Ours is not a caravan of despair.
> Come even if you have broken your vows a thousand times,
> Come, yet again, come, come.

Act

1. Describe the characteristics of having a healthy personal relationship with money. Describe the characteristics of a healthy relationship with money for your family and your faith community. Identify which characteristics you see in your personal life, your family life, and the life of your faith community. Then, identify which of these characteristics you would like to strive

for, and schedule a conversation with a family member, friend, or colleague to discuss.

2. Set aside time to talk with a trusted friend or family member about how you have experienced pain around money. Ask your friend or family member if he or she would feel comfortable sharing as well. Revisit your answers from your journal on day one of this week to use as a guide.

3. If you have not done so recently, conclude this week by giving a financial gift to the organization for which you are fundraising or to another cause close to your heart.

Week Two Touchstones

1. I understand that my relationship to money impacts my role as a fundraiser, and I commit myself to becoming more conscious of how I think about and relate to money.

2. I keep my faith in God active and alive through regular prayer and spending time with others in community.

3. I am committed to a personal practice of financial giving by thoughtfully investing in works of love and justice that inspire me.

4. I am committed to overcoming the taboo nature of talking about money. I will initiate conversations with people I trust about my own journey with money and ask about theirs.

5. I am willing to be converted from my prejudices and judgments of all people, regardless of their access to financial wealth.

6. As a fundraiser, I hold deep respect for the human need for security and the human experience of vulnerability.

WEEK THREE
Asking

Asking people for money is giving them the opportunity to put their resources at the disposal of the kingdom. To raise funds is to offer people the chance to invest what they have in the work of God.

—A Spirituality of Fundraising

Asking for money touches both our interior and exterior lives. Henri's deepest concern for fundraisers is that we have the inner freedom to be able to ask people for money. He challenges us to align our inner lives—our thoughts and emotions—with our external actions to create a stance from which we can ask for money. Henri would agree with the Trappist monk Thomas Merton, who wrote that when we try to act in the world without "deepening our own self-understanding, freedom, integrity, and capacity to love," we will ultimately transmit to others the "contagion of our own obsessions, our aggressivity, our ego-centered ambitions, our delusions about ends and means."[1] Henri explicitly conveys that our best efforts to hide feelings of jealousy or judgment toward people who have money will fail. If our invitation to people to participate in our mission is not free from anxiety, judgment, or jealousy, then it "no longer speaks in the name of God."[2]

Week Three Goal

To explore the core dynamics of asking for money

Henri does not suggest that fundraisers need to be perfect. But we do need to be on a conscious journey to grow in our inner freedom. We are not alone on this journey. But we cannot bring healing into the world, which is the ultimate goal of fundraising, without healing our inner world. The inner and the outer movements of our lives—and of the world as a whole—are inextricably linked. Each is part of the larger whole. With this understanding, asking for money becomes an opportunity to integrate mind and heart, the interior and the exterior, the spiritual and the material.

Asking for money is not easy. Many organizations and faith communities lack the funds they need because they do not ask effectively. And the inability to ask effectively is one the major reasons that paid fundraisers sometimes are not successful in their roles. Knowing this, my friends at the Suddes Group have structured their fundraising training and consultancy practice around two words: *Just ask.* In their view, these two words convey 90 percent of what we need to know about raising money. Because of anxiety, resistance, and a lack of confidence, volunteers and paid fundraisers alike—whether consciously or unconsciously—busy themselves with activities such as creating fancy websites or handouts, planning events, or doing research to avoid asking for money. None of these tasks is wrong, but, in the end, fundraising is very simple. Fundraising requires that someone ask someone else for money. It is about offering people the opportunity to become financial partners. As Henri writes, it is offering people "the chance to invest what they have in the work of God."[3]

A lot of the anxiety we have about asking for money comes from viewing "the ask" as an isolated, one-time event. Asking for money never happens in a vacuum. It always happens in the context of authentic relationships, shared

I remember clearly the first time I had lunch with a very wealthy person—an entrepreneur with a longing for justice. We had a great conversation. On the way home, I noticed I was feeling sad. It was not until the next day that I realized a part of me had been comparing myself to his financial success, leaving me a little depressed. This feeling signaled my need to go deeper in claiming my personal value and sense of worthiness.

values, a dialogue about real needs, and careful listening. Fundraising as ministry entails creating those relationships.

This week, we will reflect upon and pray with a poem I wrote.

Courage

Like a flickering candle you flare and fade.
Bless me with your fragrance.
Come to me that I may speak boldly.
Stay with me that I may rest in silence.
Inhabit me that I may trust.
Beckon me that I may return.
Feed me your wisdom that I may taste and know.

DAY ONE: THE FEAR OF ASKING

Are we willing to be converted from our fear of asking, our anxiety about being rejected or feeling humiliated, our depression when someone says, "No, I'm not going to get involved in your project"?

—*A Spirituality of Fundraising*

We all have fears, both conscious and unconscious, but the largest fear for a fundraiser may be asking for money. We know that fear sabotages opportunities in all areas of our lives, including our ability to ask for money. At the risk of oversimplifying something that can be hugely debilitating, we at least can acknowledge that fear is related to the uncertainty of outcomes. We cannot predict the future, so when we consider what will happen when we ask someone for money, it's easy to imagine the worst outcome. Money often provokes complicated emotions and core vulnerabilities. We may wonder, *What if I offend the person I am going to ask? What if my request is rejected? What if I mess up and embarrass or let down the people I am trying to serve?*

If we want to be effective in asking for money, then we must learn how to become less fearful. This has been a personal challenge for me. Some of the qualities and skills that lead to successful fundraising come easy to me, but I have always experienced "asking anxiety." And I have learned to live with it. My fear has not kept me from asking. For me, thinking about my fear just makes it grow. However, once I find myself asking, my fear subsides. This tells me that while thinking about asking increases fear, taking action reduces it. Here are three simple practices that have made a huge difference for me:

- **I try to stay emotionally connected to the people with whom and for whom I work.** If I become emotionally or intellectually disconnected from my people or the funding priorities I present to others, my anxiety and fear will escalate. Each fundraiser must find ways to be connected to the love and justice that motivates his or her fundraising.

- **I continue to practice asking—even amid my fear.** Recently, I taught a friend how to downhill ski. The first time he and I stood on the top of the hill, he felt anxious and fearful. His first several runs down the ski hill were not pretty. But he quickly gained confidence and became less fearful. Action reduces fear. Alex Honnold is one of the world's best free solo rock climbers. He climbs massive mountain faces by himself without ropes. Each time he embarks upon a climb, he knows that if he makes a mistake he will die. He works through his fear by practicing over and over and over. The more he practices, the more confident and less fearful he becomes. Action increases confidence.

- **I try to remain authentic.** The principle of authenticity means that I can acknowledge my fear of asking not only to myself but also to the people whom I am asking. Rather than letting my fear be a source of embarrassment or something I must hide, I share my fear, allowing my emotional honesty to connect me with my dialogue partner. Sharing my fear might look something like this: "Sandra, I want to tell you that I am nervous right now. Whenever I put my fundraising hat on, I get anxious. But this work is so important that I want to have this conversation with you. Can we talk about money?"

Listen

Sit silently for five to ten minutes, and listen for what today's reading has stirred within your heart. What energized you? What challenged you?

Journal

1. Name one or two people who have inspired your vision and who compel you to your mission. Practice briefly telling the story of who they are and why they matter to you. This story will ground your asking.

2. What has helped you become less fearful in other life situations? How can you use what you already know to overcome fears about asking? What are the blocks or fears that arise when you think about asking someone for money? What connections can you make between these blocks and the understandings that emerged from exploring your relationship with money?

DAY TWO: A CLEAR AND ATTRACTIVE VISION

Fundraising is precisely the opposite of begging. When we seek to raise funds we are not saying, "Please, could you help us out because lately it's been hard." Rather, we are declaring, "We have a vision that is amazing and exciting. We are inviting you to invest yourself through the resources that God has given you—your energy, your prayers, and your money—in this work to which God has called us."

—A Spirituality of Fundraising

We need a clear vision about how we are going to make an impact. If we lack a clear vision of where we want to go and how we are going to get there, we are like a rudderless boat. We will end up somewhere, perhaps in a place far from where we intended, but it is more likely that we will be washed up on a remote shore or completely shipwrecked.

Vision is central to raising money. When, like artists, we can paint a picture that connects our vision with people's minds and hearts, we can successfully build and strengthen the community of friends who will financially invest in our mission. The people who agree to becoming our funding partners will be drawn to our vision because of shared values, because of our passion, and because of how we reached out to engage them.

We need a clear, well-written vision statement. It should not be long. The implementation plan of said vision statement also should be short and specific, allowing potential donors to know how funds will be used. Even people who are close to our mission will hesitate to become involved financially if our vision is unclear. That's how important vision is to our work as fundraisers.

So how do we create a stronger and clearer vision of what we want to accomplish? And how do we develop the steps that need to be taken to make our vision a reality? There are many tools available to help us articulate our vision and objectives. Agencies and consultancies exist to help people from all walks of life do this work. The tools we use to build our vision are less important than bringing together everyone who cares about the success of the organization, whether that be three people or 300. The goal is that our community be confident and unified about its vision and action plan.

Here are some prompts to get started:

- What difference does your group want to make?
- Who will be impacted by the change you want to help bring about?
- What activities do you need to undertake to achieve your goals?
- What financial resources do you need?
- How, specifically, will you spend the money you need?
- How will your group build upon its strengths and fill in the gaps where there are weaknesses?
- What obstacles prevent you from accomplishing your mission?
- Who else shares your concerns and goals? If you are not collaborating with them already, why not?
- What will happen if you and your group do not act? Who will be affected?
- What measurable indicators of change are you working toward?
- How do you define success?

A lack of clarity about vision and the process of making it real will be a roadblock both for us (we will not want to ask) and for potential funders (they will not want to invest financially). Arriving at a simple, clear statement of vision and a plan for how we are going to move toward that vision over a specified period takes time. It's not enough to tell potential partners that we are good people, full of love, and committed to doing great things. We need a vision, a plan, and a story into which we can invite others. Then, and only then, can we start talking about it.

Listen

Sit silently for five to ten minutes, and listen for what today's reading has stirred within your heart. What energized you? What challenged you?

Journal

1. What is your compelling vision? What do you want for the future that matters so much that you are willing to give your time and energy and step out of your comfort zone to ask for money?

2. What images will convey the passion for your vision to potential funders? How might you make those images accessible to others through words, pictures, and other visuals?

DAY THREE: NO SURPRISES

If our security is totally in God, then we are free to ask for money.

—*A Spirituality of Fundraising*

No one likes to be surprised in a manner that causes embarrassment. I have never surprised someone by asking him or her for money when he or she was not expecting it. Knowing that the person I am dialoguing with about money has agreed to have such a conversation gives me confidence. The precondition for asking anyone for money is that he or she has agreed to be asked. (This does not mean, of course, that he or she has agreed to give.) Asking someone if we can "ask" is only appropriate once we know, through conversation or reputation, that shared values exist between our project and the person we want to engage. These shared values must be evident.

For example, after getting to know a potential donor's interests, I might say, "It's been great to talk with you about your personal commitment to middle school children and to get your ideas on the programs that we are developing. Would you be open to a conversation about becoming one of our financial partners? I'd love to show you our revenue plan and talk with you about how you might participate. Is that a conversation we could have?" I don't know if this potential partner will make a financial commitment or not. But the point is to ask for permission before I ask. More than anything else, embracing and integrating the principle of "no surprises" has given me confidence because I know that this practice respects the person with whom I am in relationship.

Listen

Sit silently for five to ten minutes, and listen for what today's reading has stirred within your heart. What energized you? What challenged you?

Journal

1. As you imagine asking a potential funder for permission to talk about the financial needs of your organization, how do your fears about asking for money shift, change, or dissipate?

2. How might the principle of "no surprises" impact your prospective donors?

DAY FOUR: ASKING

To raise funds is to offer people the chance to invest what they have in the work of God.

—A Spirituality of Fundraising

The time has come to ask—but this asking will not be an isolated incident. We have cultivated the mindset that we are continuing a conversation that is already in progress. We've been given permission to ask. This asking is part of a privileged conversation with someone who, like us, wants to make a difference in the world. This shared human desire is part of the sacred ground on which we stand. When fear and anxiety set in, we can remind ourselves that we already have established that the person's values align with those of our organization or cause. If this weren't the case, that person would not have granted us permission to ask for money.

We also can remind ourselves that this conversation is no different from other conversations we have had with this person. Because of that, we can be ourselves. Those fundraisers who are demonstratively emotional people should continue the conversation and make the ask with that same passion. Those fundraisers who are quiet and soft-spoken should ask with that same spirit of gentleness. Remember that asking for money is always an invitation. Invitations are never demanding or entitled, and the best ones are extended as acts of love. This invitation is not about us; it is about the people and mission we care about and the person with whom we are speaking. We are intermediaries, bringing the two together for mutual good.

When the moment of asking arrives, be bold and courageous. We can look at our dialogue partner directly without shame or embarrassment because we believe our project will make the world a more loving place. In asking, we give someone else the opportunity to be part of an exciting vision, to make new relationships and connections, and to allocate a (usually) relatively small portion of his or her resources. The desire and need to rehearse the words we use to ask someone for money is both authentic and human. I invite all of us to find the right words for our specific situations. Here are a few examples of what asking might sound like:

- "Pierre and Sandra, based on the conversation we have had, would you consider making a $5,000 gift to support our refugee relocation program that will enable five families to begin a new life in our community?"
- "Mrs. Foringer, I would like to invite you and your family to make a leadership gift of $50,000 to launch our $200,000 campaign to renovate the classrooms in the local high school. Is this an investment you could make at this time?"
- "John, we are inviting everyone who cares about this ministry to make a "stretch" gift. I don't know what that amount might be for you, but our goal is $75,000. To date, we have commitments for $55,000. Would you make a financial commitment to help us reach our goal?"

Listen

Sit silently for five to ten minutes, and listen for what today's reading has stirred within your heart. What energized you? What challenged you?

Journal

1. What excites you about asking a potential partner for money? What might be blocking you? How will you address the blocks?

2. No one type of person or personality is best for fundraising. What are the strengths of your personality in relation to fundraising? What parts of your personality could get in the way of asking for money?

DAY FIVE: TAKING STOCK

Fundraising is a very rich and beautiful activity.

—A Spirituality of Fundraising

Fear is a universal human experience. Like other fears, the fear of asking for money can be reframed as an invitation. We can think of the fear as an invitation to connect even more deeply with the people we serve and with the people whom we are asking. When fear says to us, *You're not smart/capable/ good enough to ask for money*, we can reply, *Asking isn't about me. If my community or organization cannot find the financial resources it needs to fund its mission, the well-being of others will be at risk.*

A clear vision empowers us to ask. Henri speaks to this directly when he says that sometimes the "no" that we receive can invite us to "listen more deeply to the Spirit so that our asking will be clearer and our vision more attractive."[4] The dialogue with prospective partners will always be constructive in helping us to communicate our vision more clearly in the future. The principle of only asking for money when we have been given permission to do so not only respects those with whom we are speaking but also helps us to relax and focus on developing relationships where we can speak freely about mission and money. We never will raise money unless we ask, and the only way to become more confident is to do it once, then again and again and again.

I recently attended a church service where several adults were baptized. As part of this ritual, each one of them was asked to affirm his or her choice to be baptized by declaring several sentences that included the words, "I declare my courage to participate in the building of the reign of God that is in the world and in me." These words moved me deeply. In that moment, I felt compelled to declare my own courage to participate in building the reign of God in the world and in me through fundraising. Whether we are asking for money for the first time or for the hundredth time, let us walk this path with conviction and clarity. Let us build a community of love, vulnerability, and shared vision.

Pray

It's time for you to declare your courage. Spend a few minutes with your prayer for the week.

Courage

Like a flickering candle you flare and fade.
Bless me with your fragrance.
Come to me that I may speak boldly.
Stay with me that I may rest in silence.
Inhabit me that I may trust.
Beckon me that I may return.
Feed me your wisdom that I may taste and know.

Act

1. Practice asking. Meet with a friend or family member to practice different ways of asking for money. Notice what feels most authentic to you and record those ways of asking in your journal.

2. Identify a person you trust and ask him or her to support you in your asking. Talk with this person before and after you ask a potential donor for money. Before the encounter, share with your trusted person why you want to ask this donor for money, what steps you have taken to prepare (have you asked permission to ask?), and what feelings you are experiencing as you anticipate the meeting. After the meeting, debrief with your trusted person. Talk about what worked, what felt challenging, what you might like to do differently next time, and what you are grateful for.

Week Three Touchstones

1. I invite potential financial partners to invest in a specific mission that helps build a stronger community of love in the world.

2. I trust that the Spirit who guides me is also guiding the men and women whom I ask to donate.

3. I ask potential financial partners for permission to ask them for money before I ask them for a donation.

4. I can move through my fear of asking for money by remembering why the mission of my organization and those who benefit from its work are so important.

5. I bring my authentic self to meetings with potential donors and share with them when I'm feeling nervous.

6. I am willing to get out of my head and just ask.

Creating a New Communion

When fundraising as ministry calls people together in communion with God and with one another, it must hold out the real possibility of friendship and community.

—A Spirituality of Fundraising

Two of our greatest human needs are connection and intimacy—whether with other people or with God. When Henri wrote of creating a new communion, he was referring to a coming together of like minds and spirits. Community is the concrete expression of communion. Community may take the form of a group working together for a common cause or belief system. This community may be visible and tangible to others, as in a L'Arche community or a refugee center. Or it may be virtual, expressed through online support groups, blogs, or forums. Strong bonds of friendship and support can develop even across thousands of miles.

Fundraising as ministry is grounded in our human need for communion and community. Communities are places of growth where encouragement can be given and received and where challenges can be shared. Knowing the importance of human connection, my invitation to

Week Four Goal

To explore how community both undergirds and grows out of the practice of fundraising as ministry others to join and support a community and invest financially is always part of an invitation to deepen our relationship around a shared mission.

Our human need for authentic belonging is fundamental and precious. Henri reminds us that the process of asking for money must always foster and support the creation of a "new communion." This means that *how* we raise money matters. Henri addresses this in a beautiful manner when he writes that productivity, efficiency, and profit are never an end in and of themselves. Instead, "they are only by-products of a deeper creative energy."[1] This deeper creative energy is love, which is planted and nurtured in the lives of others through the quality of our relationships. As Henri tells us, "Every time we approach someone for money, we must be sure that we are inviting them into this vision of fruitfulness."[2]

Fundraisers are gardeners, community-builders, and askers. As gardeners, we plant and nurture love. As community-builders, we offer people an opportunity to become part of our mission in whatever way works for them. As askers, we invite people to become valued partners with us to bring about wholeness and healing through clearly defined goals.

When fundraisers forget the importance of relationship and creating community, they may begin to see money as a commodity and donors as a means by which they meet fundraising goals. Over the years, I have often heard fundraisers say, "Those people have a lot of money. It would be easy for them to give us a few thousand." I have seen organizations and churches that declare themselves as donor-centric but act in ways that contradict that assertion. Money is not a commodity. Giving and investing money are expressions of the lives and values of the people with whom we partner. Our invitation is not, "Can you give us some money?" Rather, it is, "Will you partner with us? Can we deepen our relationship with you so that together we can bring more love and justice into the world? Will you generously invest and help us to raise the funds needed to make the change to which we are committed?"

Fundraisers must ask for money boldly within this context of inviting partners to join and build community. When we notice that we are feeling anxious or beginning to think more about the money than the person, we need to pause and take time to recalibrate. When we choose to see fundraising as ministry, we must remain attentive to the danger of allowing the need for money to eclipse the quality of our relationships. Fundraising as ministry never looks at a person and only sees dollar signs. The invitation to become part of a "new communion" and the offer of community and relationship is always paramount. Additionally, we also must acknowledge our need as fundraisers to be in community and to have trusted friends with whom our personal growth is encouraged and supported.

Clearly, fundraising as ministry requires asking for money. We need money in order to fulfill our mission. But we also are called to be prophetic in the sense of standing for love and justice in all that we say and do. We act prophetically when we challenge ourselves and others to nurture a vision of a better world with all our mind, heart, and strength. This vision includes living in solidarity with those who suffer, working to change systems that cause and perpetuate human suffering, and building inclusive community. We ask people to become financial partners so that together we can bring healing and wholeness into the world. Our request for money includes an invitation to join us in our prophetic work. And as members of our community, our financial partners should experience the same opportunity to live prophetically. They also should experience the love, care, affirmation, and challenge that come with being part of a heathy community.

Ultimately, Henri believed that if asking for money is not good for our spiritual lives as fundraisers or for the spiritual lives of the people we ask, then our fundraising is not ministry. Holding this belief as a core principle of our fundraising efforts will ensure that the quality of our relationships with potential partners always trumps our need for money. Fundraising is not about "closing the deal." It is about forming relationships and creating community around a shared vision to change the world.

For this final week, we will pray using a short text that Henri wrote many years ago:

> The love of God, neighbour, and self is one love. . . . This unity can be seen in three ways. First, when we direct our whole beings toward God, we will find our neighbour and ourselves right in the heart of God. Second, when we truly love ourselves as God's beloved children, we will find ourselves in complete unity with our neighbour and with God. Third, when we truly love our neighbour as our brother and sister, we will find, right there, God and ourselves in complete unity. There really is no first, second, and third in the great commandment. All is one: the heart of God, the hearts of all people, our own hearts. All the great mystics have "seen" this and lived it.[3]

DAY ONE: DEEP LONGING

[The groaning deep within us] is the sound of our yearning for communion with God and with one another, a communion that transcends the limitations of time and space.

—*A Spirituality of Fundraising*

To be human is to know and experience loneliness and, in that loneliness, the longing for connection and communion. Some of the most soulful, simple, and compassionate people I know are financially wealthy and, like me, have a longing for love, friendship, community, and communion. Some of my most generous friends are people with an intellectual disability who have no money and who experience an almost unthinkable vulnerability in our modern world. They, like me, long for friendship and communion.

One of the myths we tell ourselves about money is that money will bring us happiness. Years ago, someone with a lot of financial wealth said to me, "You know, don't you, that people who have money are neither less lonely nor happier than others? We are just more comfortable." My superficial response was to smile and nod. When I realized he was not making a joke, I replied, "Tell me more." We had a short but heartfelt encounter in which he shared some of his loneliness. I could connect with him because I too know about loneliness.

All of us—regardless of our financial status, age, ethnic or religious background, ability or disability—have a deep longing. Our longing for love and belonging is bound up with what it means to be human. As fundraisers, we may not speak explicitly about longing with our potential funding partners, but we must remember that it is the common ground upon which we stand.

Every time we begin a conversation with someone, we can remind ourselves that this person has the same deep longings that we do. He or she, like us, needs friendship, companionship, community, and communion. Does that mean that this person will or should become a financial partner? Not necessarily. But our common longing and need for community provides an immediate place of connection.

Listen

Sit silently for five to ten minutes, and listen for what today's reading has stirred within your heart. What energized you? What challenged you?

Journal

1. Where in your life are you most aware of your longing for love and community? How does that longing manifest itself?

2. How do your perceptions of potential donors change when you focus your attention on their longing for communion?

DAY TWO: THE GIFT OF COMMUNITY

People have such a need for friendship and for community that fund-raising has to be community-building.

—A Spirituality of Fundraising

Fundraising as ministry calls us to be grounded in a vision and practice of community. To grow and thrive in the work of fundraising is to embrace the double challenge of living in community while engaging in fundraising as a way to build community. Fundraising as ministry invites people into relationship, meaning approaching and viewing others as prospective members of our extended community and not as financial transactions. In this way, we invite people into a community that offers a place of belonging in the world, enables growth, and helps accomplish goals that cannot be met alone. Fundraising is about helping love and justice grow in our world by bringing people together around a common mission. We seek to build communities that say no to the myth of scarcity and yes to the reality that we live in an abundant world. As fundraisers, we invest our own money and call others to invest their money in ways that express and help actualize our core value of community.

Most people belong to more than one community. For example, I belong to the following communities: my family, my parish, my men's group of twenty years, and L'Arche, my primary place of mission for many years. Each community propels me into the heart of what I understand to be the human journey: to become more fully the person I was created to be and to make a modest contribution toward building an expansive and inclusive community of love in the world. Community helps me to be present to the joy and suffering in the world and to learn how to welcome both.

Community does not just happen. It requires intentionality, commitment, and an enormous amount of humility. A healthy community gives us a place of belonging so that we can live in such a way that benefits us and others. It's where we create bonds with others and where we give and receive love. In community, we can share our weaknesses and vulnerability and ask others to accept us as we are; we can be "real." Community is a place of creativity, innovation, and problem-solving.

As fundraisers, it is our task to announce a vision of community. If we are to do this with joy and integrity, all of us involved in fundraising need to be fed by authentic experiences of community. We need partners and friends, both within our organizations and beyond, who will join our community of love. My communities help me to be an excellent fundraiser with the utmost integrity. Within these communities, I have supportive leadership, colleagues who connect with me at the heart level as well as at the numbers level, a coach or mentor who knows me and believes in me, and trustworthy people with whom I can share and dialogue about my fundraising experiences and my questions of life and faith. My communities help me to accept the fragility of life and the discrepancy between my ideals and painful realities. My communities encourage me to persevere in difficult situations and to discern a way forward in relation to my core values. Being too alone or isolated in my role can lead to discouragement or depression. I need to be engaged in meaningful ways with others who hold and carry the mission with me. Lack of community contributes significantly to the high rate of turnover among paid fundraisers. Without a meaningful experience of community, no matter how small, fundraisers will resign from their work in frustration. That's how important community is for fundraisers and for those whom they have committed to serve.

Additionally, I would be remiss not to mention the pitfalls and pain that come from trying to create community. If we have taken on the task of fundraising, then we may describe ourselves as idealistic. And that is good because we need to have ideals that propel us forward. But our idealism may block us from embracing the reality of our messy human condition. We must acknowledge that creating an authentic community can be difficult and sometimes elusive. We all have experienced endings in relationships, friendships, or communities. If community has been the place of joy, liberation, and deep connection for us, it has also likely been the place where we have experienced some of our deepest suffering. Even so, our goal is never to stop believing in the power of community as a place of transformation.

Listen

Sit silently for five to ten minutes, and listen for what today's reading has stirred within your heart. What energized you? What challenged you?

Journal

1. Describe the different communities of which you are a member—these can be personal or professional communities. In what ways can you work to strengthen these communities and/or create a shared mission and vision?

2. As a fundraiser, how can you invite potential donors into a lived experience of community?

DAY THREE: THE DISCIPLINE OF PRAYER

Prayer is the radical starting point of fundraising because in prayer we slowly experience a reorientation of all our thoughts and feelings about ourselves and others.

—A Spirituality of Fundraising

Henri poses two key questions to people who are willing to serve others through fundraising: "How do we become people whose security base is God and God alone?"[4] and "How can we ask for money without pleading, and call people to a new communion without coercing?"[5]

His answer is that our lives must be rooted in the spiritual discipline of prayer. Throughout his writing, Henri most often speaks about prayer as listening for the small intimate voice saying, "You are my beloved Child, on you my favor rests." Prayer is not primarily the words that we offer to God or a set of activities or rituals, although it can and does include these characteristics. In essence, prayer is listening for what Henri calls the "inner voice of

To live a spiritual life, we must first find the courage to enter into the desert of our loneliness and to change it by gentle and persistent efforts into a garden of solitude. . . . The movement from loneliness to solitude, however, is the beginning of any spiritual life because it is a movement from the restless senses to the restful spirit, from the outward-reaching cravings to the inward-reaching search, from the fearful clinging to the fearless play.

—Reaching Out

love," hearing the voice, and then choosing to root our lives in the truth that we are completely and unconditionally loved.

But how can we listen for the "inner voice of love" in prayer amid a noisy and chaotic world? Henri joins spiritual leaders from many traditions in stating emphatically that the only way to prioritize an intimate relationship with God is through solitude. Solitude is much more than being alone. It is being apart from people with the intention of becoming quiet and still. It is creating space to listen to our heart, to be present to our soul, to the life within. But "Take time for solitude" will not likely show up in any job description of a volunteer or paid fundraiser. Still, Henri invites us to make solitude a priority—especially solitude rooted in prayer. Making time for times of solitude steeped in prayer requires discipline. Henri was also deeply convinced that prayer only happens through ongoing, renewable choices. In one of his earliest books, *Clowning in Rome*, he explains, "Discipline means that something very specific and concrete needs to be done to create the context in which a life of uninterrupted prayer can develop."[6]

There are many ways to practice prayer and solitude. Each person must determine what works best for his or her life and personality. I choose to practice prayer and solitude in fifteen-minute blocks, three or four times a week, but this schedule may not work for everyone. My conception and experience of God may be quite different from how others experience God. But my practice will only develop through focus and choice, and this is true for everyone. A practice can be learned and a habit formed, but most people require community support and accountability to make a new practice a way of life.

I cannot stress enough how important prayer is to the work of fundraising. It engenders trust in the whole process of fundraising. Prayer creates a space and a disposition where we can lift up all that we have—our strengths and weaknesses, our community, our mission, the people we have vowed to serve, our dreams and disappointments, those with whom we work, and all our current and potential partners—to God. "In prayer," Henri writes, "we learn to trust that God can work fruitfully through us no matter where we are or who we are with."[7] By becoming still and quiet, we can recognize and let go of our anxieties and fears. By taking time apart from others in mindful solitude, we can remind ourselves that we have enough and that we are enough. Prayer allows us to step away from our roles and goals and to know, yet again, that we belong to God. Prayer is also the place where new life, new ideas and approaches, and the desire to forgive or be forgiven will emerge, generating insight and creativity.

Listen

Sit silently for five to ten minutes, and listen for what today's reading has stirred within your heart. What energized you? What challenged you?

Journal

1. How does describing prayer as listening for the "inner voice of love" change the way you view prayer? What has prayer been for you in the past? What might shift for you if you begin to approach prayer as Henri imagined it?

2. What is your relationship to solitude? How often do you take time to sit in solitude? If you find practicing solitude to be difficult, consider why it feels challenging.

DAY FOUR: THE SPIRIT OF GRATITUDE

When we approach fundraising in a spirit of gratitude, we do so knowing that God has already given us what we most need for life in abundance.

—A Spirituality of Fundraising

Henri ends *A Spirituality of Fundraising* with a beautiful description of how gratitude is one of the signs that the process of conversion is spreading into all aspects of our lives. For fundraisers, this means not only a deepening gratitude for life as a gift to be received and shared but also an increasing freedom in our relationship to money. My fundraising activities have been huge catalysts for exploring the role of gratitude in my life. But, for me at least, being intentional about gratitude did not immediately translate into increased gratitude.

I believe in gratitude as a worldview. In the core of who I am, I know that life is a gift. I have felt gratitude bubbling up from somewhere deep within me. But more often, I am distant and detached from this good feeling. I feel as though I am looking through a window, separated from gratitude. I can still see and function, but the stress of life too often obstructs the joy and purity of heart for which I long. Fear, impatience, anger, and anxiety seem to flow so much more easily than gratitude. If I could ask Henri why gratitude is so difficult to cultivate, I imagine he would encourage me in the following ways:

- **Show up in community.** Henri might smile and say, "Yes, cultivating gratitude is hard, but let's be grateful right now, together. And let's support each other. None of us can achieve a life of gratitude alone." He would invite me to share about my relationships and would ask me where I am experiencing love and community. He certainly would pick up on the fact that for various reasons I have been much less connected to deep and meaningful community in the past several years and would encourage me to make some new choices. Henri would remind me that gratitude needs the good soil of community to grow. He might also point out how today's society can leave so many of us feeling isolated, which inevitably undermines gratitude. Since fundraising from a place of isolation is not sustainable, I must ask myself, *What changes will I make if want a fuller measure of gratitude in my life? How will I seek out community?*

- **Act with discipline.** Although gratitude can and does flow spontaneously, Henri would undoubtedly talk to me about gratitude as a spiritual discipline and connect it to the spiritual disciplines of solitude, prayer, community, and mission. Henri would advise that waiting for gratitude to arise consistently and spontaneously may not be the best path. Like silence, exercise, prayer, or study, the discipline of gratitude requires choice and explicit effort. Cultivating gratitude without a commitment to discipline won't work.

- **Fundraising is a gift.** If I shared with Henri the ups and downs of my work as a fundraiser, his eyes would begin to sparkle with the excitement of possibility. "You have a wonderful role. You are in the best situation!" he might say. "The people with whom you are working, the people you are meeting, and the conversations you are having about mission and money are opportunities for fruitful ministry. Trust this and keep going. Stay faithful to the journey you are on, and you will discover that you are becoming an ever more grateful person. Let your mission, the people with whom you share communion, and your responsibilities help you to discover the gift of life amid your work."

Listen

Sit silently for five to ten minutes, and listen for what today's reading has stirred within your heart. What energized you? What challenged you?

Journal

1. What blocks you from accessing or expressing gratitude in your fundraising and in your life? Which of Henri's three imagined responses speaks most directly to combatting those blocks?

2. How will you cultivate your capacity to live from a place of gratitude?

DAY FIVE: TAKING STOCK

Fundraising is a confident, joyful, and hope-filled expression of ministry.

—A Spirituality of Fundraising

The spiritual life, Henri often said, is lived out through the disciplines of solitude, community, and ministry. Based on the example of how Jesus lived his life, Henri observed that we usually embrace these disciplines in the wrong order. Many of us want to act, to be a loving presence in the world through ministry of one type or another. We want to make a contribution, maybe even a difference, and so we get busy doing many things. When we get tired or burned out, we realize we need community, and so we reach out to others for support. Then, when community becomes difficult (as it always does), we might take our longing and thirst to God through solitude, stillness, and prayer.

Fundraising as ministry requires that we embrace the disciplines of solitude, community, and ministry—in that order. Of course, we do not live them in a linear fashion. The three disciplines coexist, each drawing from and feeding the others. Still, Henri was convinced that our profound longing and need for solitude needs to be attended to before anything else. We ignore this need at the peril of all that matters to us. We first need to know who we are and where we belong. Then, rooted in the deep inner place where we know that we are enough and have enough, we can reach out to live the discipline of community. We can find a people with whom we can journey. Only then, with the support of others, can we actively work to build the community of love in the specific way that is right for us at any given time. Only then should we embrace the ministry for which we have been gifted.

Whether we are asking for money or giving of our resources, our essential task is to build communities of love. There are as many ways to do this as there are people in the world. But one thing is clear: This work always involves transforming the isolation, disconnection, and self-interest that we see in us and around us into connection, community, and compassion. Henri's guidance is this: "If we ask for money, it means that we offer a new fellowship, a new brotherhood, a new sisterhood, a new way of belonging. . . . Fundraising must always aim to create new, lasting relationships."[8]

The key to creating this new fellowship is understanding that money is an expression of each person's life energy and that the process of asking for money involves the spiritual task of dialoguing with people about how they are "spending" their lives. Asking for money can be reduced to a transactional experience, or it can be viewed as a way of inspiring others to lean into and discern the fullest expression of their humanity. This view of fundraising is, perhaps, a lofty one, but how we frame our work is extremely important. Fundraising is messy—as messy as life itself—because we are working with people and also trying to make sense of our own preconceived notions of money and those who have money. Our call as fundraisers is not to be perfect. Our call is to live, pray, and build community from a spirit of gratitude and abundance. We cannot focus on our faults and weaknesses or those of others; instead, let us focus on drawing out the best of each person and the best of each community so that we can live into the fullness of life.

Pray

Again, spend time in prayer, reflecting on Henri's text below.

> The love of God, neighbour, and self is one love. . . . This unity can be seen in three ways. First, when we direct our whole beings toward God, we will find our neighbour and ourselves right in the heart of God. Second, when we truly love ourselves as God's beloved children, we will find ourselves in complete unity with our neighbour and with God. Third, when we truly love our neighbour as our brother and sister, we will find, right there, God and ourselves in complete unity.

There really is no first, second, and third in the great commandment.
All is one: the heart of God, the hearts of all people, our own hearts.
All the great mystics have "seen" this and lived it.

Act

1. Think back over what you have learned over the past four weeks. With
   Henri's view of fundraising as ministry in mind, declare your core values.
   What commitments do you make to yourself, to your community, and to
   those with whom you will dialogue about money?

2. Choose two people with whom you will share your core values. Ask for their
   encouragement and for them to consider joining you in community around
   your mission.

Week Four Touchstones

1. I invite people into relationship and community when I ask them to become financial partners.

2. I invite donors into a vision that is fruitful, and I plant and nourish seeds of love in them and in the lives of those I serve.

3. I am attentive to the danger of allowing the need for money to eclipse the quality of the relationships I build with potential donors.

4. I approach meetings with potential financial partners with an awareness that we stand together on the common ground of our longing for connection and community.

5. I commit myself to setting aside time regularly to listen for the inner voice of love, anchoring myself in the truth that I am loved unconditionally.

6. I practice the discipline of gratitude by giving heartfelt thanks to God for my life and for those close to me, by expressing gratitude to others verbally, and by the gestures that are true for me and those who are with me on life's journey.

CONCLUSION

We've come to the end of our journey with Henri's inspiring and energizing vision of fundraising as ministry. But, of course, our work only is just beginning. What now? We do not have to look very far to discover that fundraising is everywhere. It involves people from all walks of life who are connected to countless types of organizations, schools, churches, religious communities, and social justice movements.

As fundraisers who view our work as ministry, we can affirm the following:

- We believe in abundance.
- We are willing to shed negative attitudes about fundraising.
- We are ready to move out of our comfort zone and act with the conviction of our vision.
- We accept that fundraising is inextricably linked to our relationship with money.
- We commit to becoming more personal and to be grounded in heart and spirit as we do our work.
- We desire to create a community of love.
- We vow never to let fundraising become more about money than relationships.

We all are called to give, to discover the joy of giving, and to give generously of ourselves and our resources. Moreover, we are called to discover and experience the joy of asking. Both the agony and the unbounded potential that bookend our human condition and our commitment to love and justice call us to ask for money boldly, with confidence and passion.

Henri has painted a beautiful picture of fundraising as ministry. Perhaps, if we close our eyes and use our imagination, we can see this picture. The subjects of the painting are a small group of people deeply engaged with one another and grounded in a sense of community and shared vision. We sense their unity of purpose in the intense, vibrant brushstrokes of color that harmoniously come together. Something important is taking place. Henri invites us to step into and become part of this picture—to bring our commitment and gifts into the group, to contribute to and feed off the energy already in the world.

Henri once wrote that we need to "be patient and trust that the treasure we look for is hidden in the ground on which we stand."[1] The fundraising work that our communities need will not be met by some extraordinary person who has special talents. It will be met by ordinary people like us, who engage the ministry of fundraising with extraordinary love. The treasure is here—in us and around us.

It's time to be generous and brave and to trust that by working with others, we can help build the partnerships that will enable our communities to sustain the good work of their mission.

Onward!

APPENDIX 1: CREATING A FUNDRAISING JOURNAL

As you explore a spirituality of fundraising and use Henri's vision to develop or strengthen your fundraising practice, I highly recommend that you create and use a fundraising journal. Find a blank journal that appeals to you, and get started. A dedicated, personal fundraising journal can be the glue that holds together all the different parts of the fundraising process. A journal will support you as you navigate the coexisting and often opposing demands of fundraising: the demand to be present with your community and financial partners and the demand to be productive. When you take time for solitude to write in your journal, you will connect with your own belovedness, which, in turn, will help you to be present to the belovedness of others. The productivity side of fundraising will be supported as you document your priorities, change them as life unfolds, and write your plans to meet with people and follow-up on those meetings.

Try using your journal in three ways:

- **Workbook questions.** Use your journal to explore some of the questions that are posed throughout this workbook. Take time to answer the questions thoughtfully—especially the ones that pose challenges that may help you in your growth as a fundraiser.
- **Extemporaneously.** A journal is a place where you can write about and consider your fundraising journey. Take notes about what you have read and learned, doodle, dream, list your goals and intentions, map out action steps for meeting your goals, and track your progress. Document your feelings, and push yourself to think deeply about your insights and ideas.

- **Sections.** Create sections in your journal where you can home in on specific themes, activities, or goals related to your work as a fundraiser. Choose from the following possibilities or create your own:
  — My Money Autobiography
  — Naming, Exploring, and Letting Go of Fears
  — Gratitude Log
  — People Who Matter and Why
  — Priorities
  — Helpful Books and Blogs
  — Building Community
  — Insights from Time Spent in Silence and Solitude

One creative journal format that has inspired me is the Bullet Journal. You can find a short video explaining how it works at www.bulletjournal.com. The video focuses primarily on the realm of productivity, but a quick Internet search for "bullet journal images" will give you a sense of the creative ways that people use this format for journaling.

APPENDIX 2: WORKSHOP TEMPLATE

Workshops gather people together to learn about a specific topic. Properly designed workshops allow people to connect with others who are interested or working in the same field as they are. Workshops allow people to engage around new ideas and common experience. The following is a workshop template that you may consider using. If you find this template helpful, then use it as a framework for creating other short (or longer) workshops on various themes.

Title: Fundraising as Ministry

Purpose: A short, intense time of learning that can be inserted into a board meeting, a council or stewardship team meeting, or a leadership team gathering.

Goal: To explore how fundraising can be practiced as ministry. To notice roadblocks and identify possibilities for implementation.

Pre-reading: "Week One: Fundraising as Ministry" from *The Spirituality of Fundraising Workbook Edition*, pages 39–59

Time: 20–25 minutes

Materials: Flip chart and markers

The facilitator will bring the flip chart prepared in the following way: The first page of the flip chart will be blank. On the second page of the flip chart, the facilitator will write out a simple description of the schedule for the workshop (see next pages). On the third page of the flip chart, the facilitator will write the following: *Fundraising as ministry announces an inspiring vision rooted in the love of God and a desire to build community. It cannot be reduced to the process of finding cash for a mission. In fundraising as ministry, the quality of relationships for all involved is always more important than both short-term and long-term monetary results.*

The Workshop

The facilitator offers a very brief introduction to launch the workshop by going over the schedule for the day on the second page of the flip chart.

Brainstorming (3–5 minutes)

a. Divide first page of the flip chart into three sections. Facilitator says, "When I say the word *ministry*, what words or phrases come to mind?" Ask participants to call out the words, and write them in the first section.

b. After a minute or so, do the same with the word *fundraising*. "When I say the word *fundraising*, what words or phrases come to mind?" Write down the words that are called out in the second section.

c. Lastly, invite responses to the phrase *fundraising as ministry*. What shifts when we put these words together? What associations emerge? Write these in the third section.

Reflection (5–7 minutes)

a. Go to third page of the flip chart, and read the text aloud.

b. Ask the participants to stand up, move around the room, and choose a partner. Then ask them to answer the following questions with their partner:

i.   What blocks or hesitations do you experience when you reflect on this vision of fundraising as ministry?

ii. What aspects of this vision excite you?

iii. How might you see yourself participating in fundraising as ministry?

d. Debrief (3 minutes).

i.   Ask members to share what most impacted them from their conversations with their partner. Write out their responses (in abbreviated form) on the flip chart.

Next Steps (5–7 minutes)

As a group, discuss how the learning and wisdom that just emerged can be integrated into the organization's mission, vision, or ministry. If appropriate, identify two or three concrete steps, and designate persons who will take the lead on each one. Decide as a group whether you would like to study the rest of the workbook together at a later time.

NOTES

Introduction

1. Henri J. M. Nouwen, *The Way of the Heart: The Spirituality of the Desert Fathers and Mothers* (London: Darton, Longman and Todd Ltd., 1999), 66.
2. Henri J. M. Nouwen, *The Return of the Prodigal Son* (New York: Convergent Books, 2016), 229.

How to Use This Workbook

1. Henri J. M. Nouwen, *Here and Now: Living in the Spirit* (New York: The Crossroad Publishing Company, 1994), 83.

A Spirituality of Fundraising

1. Henri J. M. Nouwen, *A Spirituality of Fundraising* (Nashville, TN: Upper Room Books, 2010). Used by permission of The Henri Nouwen Legacy Trust.

Week One: Fundraising as Ministry

1. Father Kenneth Untener, "Prophets of a Future Not Our Own." This reflection is an excerpt from a homily written for John Dearden, Archbishop of Detroit, by Father Kenneth Untener on the occasion of the Mass for Deceased Priests, October 25, 1979.
2. Henri J. M. Nouwen, *The Inner Voice of Love: A Journey Through Anguish to Freedom* (New York: Image Books, 1998), 18–19.
3. Henri J. M. Nouwen, *Home Tonight: Further Reflections on the Parable of the Prodigal Son* (New York: Doubleday, 2009), 313.

4. Nouwen, *The Return of the Prodigal Son*, 313.

Week Two: Our Security Base

1. Nouwen, *The Return of the Prodigal Son*, 126–7.
2. Henri J. M. Nouwen, *Bread for the Journey: A Daybook of Wisdom and Faith* (San Francisco: HarperSanFrancisco, 1997), January 3.

Week Three: Asking

1. Thomas Merton, *Contemplation in a World of Action* (Garden City, NY: Doubleday, 1971), 164.
2. Nouwen, *A Spirituality of Fundraising*, 44.
3. Nouwen, 45–46.
4. Nouwen, 45.

Week Four: Creating a New Communion

1. Nouwen, *A Spirituality of Fundraising*, 51.
2. Nouwen, 51.
3. Rebecca Laird and Michael J. Christensen, eds., *The Heart of Henri Nouwen: His Words of Blessing* (London: Darton, Longman and Todd Ltd., 2004), 111.
4. Nouwen, *A Spirituality of Fundraising*, 55.
5. Nouwen, 55.
6. Henri J. M. Nouwen, *Clowning in Rome: Reflections on Solitude, Celibacy, Prayer, and Contemplation* (New York: Image Books, 1979), 76.
7. Nouwen, *A Spirituality of Fundraising*, 57.
8. Nouwen, 50.

Conclusion

1. Nouwen, *Bread for the Journey*, January 5.

ABOUT THE AUTHORS

Internationally renowned author, respected professor, and beloved pastor, Henri Nouwen wrote over forty books on the spiritual life that have inspired and comforted countless people throughout the world. Since his death in 1996, an ever-increasing number of readers, writers, and researchers are exploring his literary legacy. Henri Nouwen's works have been translated and published in more than twenty-two different languages.

Born in Nijkerk, Holland on January 24, 1932, Nouwen was ordained in 1957. Moved by his desire for a better understanding of human suffering, he went in 1964 to the United States to study in the Religion and Psychiatry Program at the Menninger Clinic. He went on to teach at the University of Notre Dame, the Pastoral Institute of Amsterdam, and the Divinity Schools of both Yale and Harvard, where his classes were among the most popular on campus.

Nouwen's strong appeal as a teacher and writer had much to do with his passion to integrate all aspects of his life into a lived spirituality. He was convinced that striving for such integration is an urgent need in our culture. His writing, often autobiographical, gave readers a window into the joys and struggles of their own spiritual quest. The universal character of Nouwen's spiritual vision crossed many boundaries and inspired a wide range of individuals: Wall Street bankers, politicians and professionals, Peruvian peasants, teachers, religious leaders, ministers and caregivers.

Nouwen traveled widely during his lifetime, lecturing on topics such as ministry and caregiving, compassion, peacemaking, suffering, solitude, community, dying and death.

Nouwen was always searching for new images to convey the depth of the good news of the gospel message. For example, he met and befriended a group of trapeze artists in a traveling circus. Just prior to his sudden death, he was working on a project to use life in the circus as an image of the spiritual journey. *The Return of the Prodigal Son*, one of his classic works, marries art and spirituality in a contemporary interpretation of the ancient gospel parable.

Nouwen lived the last ten years of his life with people who have developmental disabilities in a L'Arche community near Toronto, Canada.

———

Nathan Ball met and shared community life with Henri Nouwen in Jean Vanier's L'Arche community in France and Canada for over ten years. Their friendship and Nouwen's spiritual vision had a life-changing impact on Ball, who has held various leadership roles within the L'Arche movement. He was a founding trustee of the Henri Nouwen Legacy Trust and was on the board of directors of the Henri Nouwen Society for several years. For the past twenty years, he has been heavily involved in various aspects of fundraising. Ball now lives in St. Louis, Missouri.